071 BA7A

1945—

Fredrik Chr. Brøgger

Culture, Language, Text

For *Ellen, Marianne,* and *Synnøve*

Fredrik Chr. Brøgger

Culture, Language, Text:
Culture Studies within the Study of English as a Foreign Language

Scandinavian University Press

Scandinavian University Press (Universitetsforlaget AS), 0608 Oslo
Distributed world-wide excluding Norway by
Oxford University Press, Walton Street, Oxford OX2 6DP

London New York Toronto
Delhi Bombay Calcutta Madras Karachi
Kuala Lumpur Singapore Hong Kong Tokyo
Nairobi Dar es Salaam Cape Town
Melbourne Auckland

and associated companies in
Beirut Berlin Ibadan Mexico City Nicosia

© Universitetsforlaget AS 1992

Cover design by Ellen Larsen

Published with a grant from the Norwegian Research Council for Science and the Humanities

All rights reserved. No part of this publication may be reproduced, stored in a retrieval system, or transmitted, in any form or by any means, electronic, mechanical, photocopying, recording, or otherwise, without the prior permission of Scandinavian University Press (Universitetsforlaget AS)

British Library Cataloguing in Publication Data

Brogger, Fredrik Christian, *1945* –
  Culture, language, text: culture studies within
  the study of English as a foreign language.
  306.4

ISBN 82-00-02942-5

Printed in Norway by Tangen Grafiske Senter AS, Drammen 1992

973.071 B674c

Brøgger, Fredrik Chr. 1945–

Culture, language, text

Contents

ACKNOWLEDGEMENTS 9

INTRODUCTION 10
Main Aims and Intended Audience 10
Culture as a Theoretical Nucleus for Interdisciplinarity 11
Notes 14

CHAPTER 1: THE TERM USED TO BE «BACKGROUND»:
CULTURE STUDIES AS A LAISSEZ-FAIRE DISCIPLINE 15
Notes 18

CHAPTER 2: A NATIVE MODEL:
CULTURE STUDIES AS AN AMERICAN STUDIES
DISCIPLINE 19
The Myth-and-Symbol School 20
Multidisciplinary vs. Interdisciplinary American Studies 21
Towards an American *Culture* Studies 25
Notes 28

CHAPTER 3: THE STUDY OF DOMINANT ASSUMPTIONS
AND VALUES:
CULTURE STUDIES AS AN ANTHROPOLOGICAL
DISCIPLINE 31
Culture Conceived as Belief Systems 32
Conceptions of Culture: Unity vs. Diversity 33
Definition of the Discipline of Culture Studies 37
A Culture Studies Analysis of a Text 40
Notes 43

CHAPTER 4: CULTURE AND LANGUAGE:
CULTURE STUDIES AS A LINGUISTICS DISCIPLINE 46
Contextual Linguistic Theories 47
Towards a Cultural Syntactics and Morphology 49

Towards a Cultural Pragmatics and Semantics 55
Towards a Cultural Discourse Analysis 58
Notes 61

CHAPTER 5: THE «LITERARINESS» OF ORDINARY
LANGUAGE:
CULTURE STUDIES AS A LITERARY-ORIENTED
DISCIPLINE 62
"Literary" vs. "Ordinary" Language.. 62
Cultural Simile, Metaphor, Symbol... 65
Cultural Narrative 68
Three Cultural Texts Analyzed in Literary Terms 69
Notes 76

CHAPTER 6: CULTURE, HISTORY, AND INTERPRETATION:
CULTURE STUDIES AS A HISTORICAL DISCIPLINE 78
Explanation vs. Interpretation... 78
Referentiality vs. Figurativeness 80
"Fact" vs. "Fiction" 82
The Particular vs. the Representative 86
Notes 91

CHAPTER 7: CULTURE AND TEXT:
CULTURE STUDIES AS A PHILOLOGICAL DISCIPLINE 93
The Nature of Philology 93
A Philological Analysis of a Text.. 94
Some Reservations About Cultural Generalizations 98
Notes 100

CHAPTER 8: CULTURE AND THE CLASSROOM:
CULTURE STUDIES AS A DIDACTIC DISCIPLINE 101
Four Pitfalls of the Teaching of Culture Studies 102
The Interrelations of Culture, Language, and
   Literature.. 108
The Use of Text in Teaching 110
The Three-Step Methodology of Culture Studies Teaching 112
A Culture Studies Syllabus Exemplified 115
The Teaching of Two Topics Exemplified 118
Notes 124

CHAPTER 9: THE SCHOLARSHIP OF TEXTUAL ANALYSIS:
CULTURE STUDIES AS A RESEARCH DISCIPLINE 125
"Discipline" vs. "Area of Study": The Issue of
  "Scientificness" 126
An Interdisciplinary Research Competence 127
Definition of Culture Studies as a Research Discipline 130
Culture Studies Research Exemplified 131
Notes 135

CHAPTER 10: OVERARCHING SYNTHESIS:
THE STUDY OF ENGLISH AS A WHOLE 136
Some Modest Didactic Proposals 136
The Need for a Research Commitment
  to Interdisciplinarity 137

BIBLIOGRAPHY: WORKS CITED 141

Acknowledgements

The subject of the theory and methodology of culture studies has occupied me, on and off, for more than a decade. It was, however, during my sabbatical at the University of California, San Diego in 1988-89 that this book was written. I would like to thank the University of Tromsø for granting the one-year sabbatical, and the Norwegian Research Council for Science and the Humanities for subsidizing parts of the extra family costs incurred by living abroad. I would also like to express my appreciation of a Fulbright research grant from the U.S. Educational Foundation and a Wigeland scholarship from the American-Scandinavian Foundation, without which I would have been unable to complete the research for this book.

When revising this book for publication, I have drawn upon helpful comments of colleagues and friends. I am particularly grateful for the response from Professor Karen Risager at Roskilde University, who read the entire manuscript on its completion. For their observations on parts or the whole of this book, I am also indebted to Ole Moen and Torbjørn Sirevåg, Professors of English (American Civilization) at the University of Oslo; Jostein Børtnes, Professor of Russian (Literature) at the University of Bergen; and Annabelle Despard, Professor of English (British Civilization) at Agder Regional College. For reading particular chapters in the manuscript, I would like to thank Leiv-Egil Breivik, Professor of English (Language) at the University of Bergen; Jan Brøgger, Professor of Social Anthropology at the University of Trondheim; and the following at the University of Tromsø: Lisbet Holtedahl, Professor of Social Anthropology; Marit Richardsen Westergaard, Professor of English (Language); and Tone Skinningsrud, Professor of Educational Research.

Last, but not least, I am grateful to Orm Øverland, Professor of English (American Literature) at the University of Bergen, who besides reading parts of my manuscript, provided me with three opportunities in the 1980s to express in public my ideas on the interconnections of language and culture, by once inviting me to write a contribution to a symposium and twice inviting me to lecture at conferences.

Introduction

This is a book about the discipline sometimes termed *culture studies* within the study of English as a foreign language. At some universities the subject is better known as the study of *civilization* (predominantly British and American). The German term often used is *Landeskunde,* the French one *civilisation,* and the Scandinavian one *kulturkunnskap* (literal translation, "knowledge of culture"). The "native" fields of study in the United Kingdom and the United States which correspond most closely to these subjects are *British Studies* and *American Studies.* These last subjects, however, usually lack the orientation towards linguistic analysis which must have priority in culture studies within the study of a foreign language.

At many universities and colleges in Scandinavia as well as abroad, the field of foreign language study consists of three subdisciplines: the studies of language, literature, and culture. Particularly in recent years, the study of the culture in which a specific language is spoken has come to be regarded as increasingly important for the understanding of that language. The discipline of culture studies contributes to the grasp and understanding of the larger culture-specific discourse that must supplement the grammatical study of isolated phrases and sentences. This concern with a larger context, also reflected in literary studies, is part of what distinguishes a university *humanities* education in foreign languages from the kind of language instruction provided by commercial language schools.

Main Aims and Intended Audience

The aim of this book is to provide the discipline of culture studies in foreign language study with a theory and a methodology of its own. Although there is considerable agreement on the need for the field of culture studies within the study of a foreign language at the university level, there is as yet little agreement on its definition and its function *vis-à-vis* the two traditional disciplines of linguistics and literary studies. How should culture studies best be defined within the framework of foreign language studies in particular and the humanities in general? What are to be the primary theoretical objectives of the discipline – its main cognitive aims? What should be its basic modes and tools of analysis? What sort of material should constitute its main object of study? How should it best be taught? What particular issues need further study and research? These are some of the central questions dealt with in this study.

This book is intended primarily for teachers and advanced students of English at universities and colleges in countries where English is not the native language. It is a response to the widespread demand among scholars of English in Scandinavia for an approach to the study of civilization evolved from the textual-linguistic character of foreign-language study itself. At the same time it is meant to meet the theoretical and methodological needs of advanced civilization students of English – graduate students as well as students attending upper division (intermediate level) courses. This book may also be of interest to teachers of English in secondary schools, providing them with ideas of how to work with cultural texts in the classroom. And finally, its emphasis on foreign language study notwithstanding, this book is written in the hope that American Studies scholars in the United States may also find some of its approaches and practices useful and interesting for their own teaching and scholarship.

At times, this book refers specifically to the study of English in Norway and Scandinavia, but its general orientation makes it relevant to the study of English at most foreign universities and colleges. Although the book is mainly about the study of *English* as a foreign language, its theoretical focus also makes its discussion applicable to culture studies within the fields of other foreign languages, be they German, Russian, or whatever. Because the subject of my own teaching and research is the culture of the United States, most of the exemplary cultural texts used for illustration in this book are American ones, but again, the general *principles* involved in foreign language study and interpretation are the same regardless of the particular cultural illustrations that are employed.

Culture as a Theoretical Nucleus for Interdisciplinarity

The concern with culture is nothing new in language studies. In the l9th century as well as in the first third of this century, the study of languages was intimately bound up with the field of *philology,* the careful historical explication and interpretation of the language of a text in terms of the age and culture to which it belonged. In philological studies there were no sharp lines of demarcation drawn between language, literature, and culture; philology represented a genuinely interdisciplinary approach to the study of texts.

With the academic specialization of our own time, however, the study of foreign languages lost much of its general, cultural orientation, particularly in the period between the 1930s and the 1960s. This development was bound up with the emergence of strictly formalist and structuralist modes of thinking. After midcentury, foreign language studies tended to embody only two main disciplines, increasingly professionalized and separate: linguistics on the one hand and literary study on the other. Both fields primarily viewed their objects of study as constituting a synchronic system; language in general, or that of a particular literary work, was regarded as an autonomous system of significations, a self-contained totality of various structural elements. The idea of the interrelations between the different disciplines was lost. Not even the subjects of language and literature were analyzed in an interdisciplinary manner so as to reveal, in theory and practice, their interconnections, as had been the case with earlier philological studies.

Since the 1970s, however, the understanding of culture has once more gained recognition as an important component of the study of a foreign language. Whether the English Department's official term is "Civilization," "British Studies"/"American Studies," or "Culture Studies," the discipline is seen to contribute to the student's communicative competence as well as to increase his analytical and interpretive understanding of linguistic-cultural discourse. Today, the field of culture studies tends to seek its inspiration not only from the cultural concerns of traditional philology, but also from the ideas of culture in the social sciences – particularly within the field of anthropology. Shaped by the needs and objectives of language study, however, the field of culture studies is neither some traditional *Geistesgeschichte* nor pure social science, but an interdisciplinary study within the humanities. The objective of this book is to define the discipline of culture studies in a systematic manner, and thus to legitimize it as an academic humanities discipline.

Such legitimation is necessary. Due to institutional pressures, the emergence of culture studies in departments of foreign language studies has often been resisted by scholars who see themselves as working strictly within the conventional boundaries of literary studies or linguistics. This defensive scholarly attitude is not only a matter of the scepticism with which newcomers are frequently regarded; it is also a product of the academic scramble for funds and positions. Such conflicts have often produced the argument that the field of culture studies has still to "prove" (to the others) its status as an academic, "scientific" subject. Typical in this connection is a passage from the 1985 *Report on Research in the Humanities in Norway,* published by the Norwegian Research Council for Science and the Humanities, suggesting that there seem "not to be sufficient grounds for presenting *culture studies* as a separate research discipline."[1] Too much research in American and British Studies had been done by the mid-1980s to warrant such a judgment. In the specialization era of the 1950s and 60s, however, even the subject of foreign language study itself failed to make manifest its own academic characteristics. At that time there was relatively little awareness of the fact that the disciplines within the study of foreign languages generate their own particular academic needs and research questions.

Just as culture studies must inevitably be defined somewhat differently within a foreign language study than within the social sciences, so too is the case with the disciplines of language and literary study. Their dominant scientific concerns must not be confused with those of general linguistics or general literature. The inherent focus engendered by language study helps shape the cognitive objectives of its linguistic, cultural, and literary components – in terms of research as well as teaching. The study of a foreign language is inherently an interdisciplinary one.

In this book, the anthropological concept of *culture* as *belief systems* serves as the theoretical nucleus of the discipline of culture studies, whose main cognitive aim consequently is the analysis of the dominant patterns of beliefs and values of a society or a social group. Concerned with the interplay between language and ideology, the field of culture studies finds its *raison d'être* in an extended concept of communication, according to which the use of language demands a cultural as well as a linguistic competence. Primarily a study of texts and the ways in which they give expression to the interconnections between language and beliefs, culture studies requires a combination of several analytical approaches from the social sciences and the humanities. The field of culture studies is thus seen as an essentially interdisciplinary venture, combining anthropological, historical, linguistic, and literary methods of analysis – hence the title of this work, *Culture, Language, Text.*

This book first discusses the origins of the discipline of culture studies within language study in Norway (Chapter 1) and within the American Studies movement in the United States (Chapter 2). It then goes on to consider what the following fields may contribute to the study of culture within the study of English as a foreign language: anthropology (Chapter 3), linguistics (Chapter 4), literary studies (Chapter 5), history (Chapter 6), and philology (Chapter 7). The two subsequent chapters discuss the endeavor of the discipline of culture studies to integrate these fields in teaching (Chapter 8) and in research (Chapter 9). The concluding chapter extends the idea of interdisciplinary synthesis to the study of English as a whole (Chapter 10).

The interdisciplinary venture of culture studies is ultimately seen to follow a three-step methodology in research as well as in teaching: from *historical and social analysis,* through the *cultural analysis* of dominant belief systems, to the *textual analysis* of the ways in which these dominant belief systems are encoded in the language of written sources. Such a procedure involves extensive use of both linguistic-philological and literary approaches to the study of texts. In this manner, it is hoped to engender a comprehensive insight into the interplay between culture and language.

This book will probably provoke some disdain among the purists of linguistics and literature in departments of English, to whom "science," "scholarship," and "research" are synonymous with work within traditional disciplinary categories. The study of a particular foreign language, however, cannot be pursued or taught from the point of view of academic compartmentalization. The future development of a study like that of English depends on systematic, scholarly inquiry into the interrelations between its three main subdisciplines of language, culture, and literature. And it is particularly within this framework that the discipline of culture studies assumes an important function.

Notes

1 *Humaniorautgreiinga: Humanistisk forsking i Noreg, del II [The Humanities Report: Humanist Research in Norway, Part II]* (Oslo: Rådet for humanistisk forsking [The Council for Research in the Humanities], NAVF, 1985), p. 12.

1
The Term used to be «Background»: Culture Studies as a Laissez-faire Discipline

If the depreciatory words of the Norwegian Humanities Report on the allegedly "unclear scientific status" of culture studies[1] had been presented in 1970 instead of 1985, they would have been perfectly justified. During my years as a university student of English in the mid and late 1960s in Norway, the subject was simply termed "Background." The name indicated that it was not considered a field in its own right, but served as an appendage of sorts, something secondary and supplementary. What it was supposed to serve as a background *to*, however, never became clear. It did not really fill out the picture for anything else on the syllabus, and whatever was foregrounded for us in our studies never seemed connected with this backdrop. Teachers of language hardly ever referred to this "Background" and teachers of literature themselves presented whatever extra-literary information they deemed necessary. "Background" teachers, in their turn, hardly ever proceeded to analyze language in their sessions, and they dealt with current affairs and institutions in ways which seemed unrelated to the approaches and techniques of literary study.

Consequently the term "Background" appeared to characterize neither the field itself nor its relationship to the other disciplines. Instead, it seemed to spring from some extra function *vis-à-vis* the students, giving *them* some "background," some additional information about the countries whose language they were studying. This type of study could perhaps be viewed as a remnant of the prespecialization ideals of a general classical education. It was, however, just as much an adjustment on the part of the university English departments to developments taking place in the Norwegian secondary schools, where non-literary, discursive material on life in Britain and America had been steadily growing at the expense of literary texts. At first consisting mainly of a brief presentation of the political institutions of the United Kingdom and the United States, university "Background" teaching in Norway soon mushroomed into a two-semester course (at the first year level only), introducing the student of English to a variety of different aspects of British and American society – for example, their regions, institutions, politics, social structure, racial and ethnic relations, religion, mass media, and educational system. The problem with this expanded version of "Background" studies, however, was that it still remained unrelated to the two other disciplines of linguistics and literary study. In the secondary school, the single teacher of English taught as if she/he were covering three essentially different subjects; and at the universities, three different teachers would present their material as if they were not dealing with the same subject of study, that of English.

Even at this stage, "Background" was therefore widely regarded as a kind of stepchild of the two other disciplines – something bothersome yet tolerated as part of the undertaking. Even language and literature teachers had in fact begun to regard, however reluctantly, some knowledge of a foreign society as important for the study of the language of that society. A general agreement was also emerging that "Background" should analyze the *general* features of American and British society – that is, what was typical and characteristic of the life of each nation. Beyond this, however, there was little agreement on the nature of this knowledge, what its primary source material should be, how it should be studied, and how it should be taught. There was, in short, an acute lack of theory.

Most teachers of "Background" tried to do both too much and too little in their teaching. They tended to do too much in the sense of trying to cover as many aspects of British and American society as possible, and too little in the sense of failing to work out any overall conception of the whys and wherefores of their own instruction. The result was a scholarly *laissez-faire*, aggravated by a feeling of helplessness *vis-à-vis* a field which appeared limitless; everything that had to do with British or American society in one way or other seemed relevant for one's teaching. At the beginning of the 1970s, "Background" teachers felt that theirs was a superhuman task – they had to play sociologist one day, historian the next, political scientist the third, and so on *ad infinitum*.

This was also the situation when I obtained my first lectureship in 1974, which specifically involved both American literature and American "Background." Having received most of my university education in literary studies, the latter field was virgin territory to me. So I dealt with "Background" in much the same way you deal with troublesome questions of etiquette at formal parties: you look at what the person next to you is doing. So I proceeded to teach "Background" the way it was being done at Norwegian universities at the time, namely as a one-year cafeteria course for first year students of English with a mishmash of dishes ranging from demography to intellectual history, from geography to popular culture.

When a course is being taught for the first time, nobody learns as much as the teacher. This was doubly true of my "Background" course, as I felt like an explorer in a strange land or, less romantically, a greenhorn away from home. Nevertheless, engrossed and exhilarated and full of misgivings, I roamed from discipline to discipline and from subject to subject: from sociology to political science; from the Other America to the Imperial Presidency; from the Organization Man to sex roles; from the Civil War to the Board of Education of Topeka; from Melting Pots to Bay of Pigs; from discussing the number of Americans believing in God to analyzing Ajax-the-white-tornado commercials... The list, in theory if not in practice, becomes inexhaustible. I was actually so preoccupied with trying to keep up with my subjects that I hardly had time to think about the nature and aim of the course itself, until a couple of my students one day confronted me with the question: "What are we actually supposed to learn from this course?" I muttered something along the line of "ehhh... importance of becoming acquainted with different aspects of American life... unhh..." "But this jumping from one topic to another," objected a third student, "is so disconnected and superficial." Later, I heard similar objections from other students, which served to reinforce my own vague but persistent misgivings about this "Background" approach. Gradually, I came to feel that my students' comments were entirely justified. Seen in retrospect, the course seemed like the academic equivalent to an early 1970s film farce about American tourists in Europe called something like *"It's Tuesday, so this must be Belgium";* only here it was more like "It's the second week of October, so today must be American education, and next week it is religion." Far from becoming a melting pot, the course represented a very mixed salad bowl indeed. Even the salad metaphor fails to do justice to this pot-pourri: it was more like mixing meat and cake and fish and ice-cream on the same plate.

"Background" was in this sense an appropriate term for the course; I came to feel that nothing justified this sort of hotchpotch teaching. I do not think this was exclusively a matter of my own professional shortcomings in dealing with these diverse subjects. The acute problem was how to integrate them. To me, the minimal requirement of a university discipline was that it had certain cognitive objectives of its own – that the study, say, of the United States, had a theory of how to systematize knowledge about American life and thus attain a methodical understanding of its typical characteristics. And the chief aim of such a general study, it seemed to me, was to explain the interconnections between various aspects of American life. I was not prepared to give up teaching this field yet. I felt that it somehow *was* of great importance for the study of English as a foreign language, and that it somehow *deserved* a place on the curriculum.

To me, then, interdisciplinarity had to be the key issue – an overarching scientific perspective for the integration of various fields of study. In this regard, the student of American life happens to have a more advantageous starting point than the students of many other cultures, because Americans have a long tradition of trying to define the characteristics of their own way of life. In contrast, Englishmen or Frenchmen, for example, have not felt the same almost obsessive urge to define their "Englishness" or "Frenchness." Being an American, however, has often been experienced as an ideological condition as much as a fact of birth; it has meant being part of a vision, and sharing (albeit in varying degrees) a world view. Precisely this concern with trying to characterize an American world view – or perhaps competing and conflicting American world views – seemed a promising direction in which to work, if at the same time due attention was paid to the heterogeneity of American life, to the cultural differences between various groups in the United States.

The most striking manifestation in the humanities of this American propensity for self-definition has been the so-called American Studies movement, which became an important field of study at many American universities in the period from the 1950s to the 70s. At the same time, American Studies had begun to focus precisely on the problems of the theory and methods of an interdisciplinary study of American life. For a "Background" teacher like me, disillusioned as I was with my own atomistic, *laissez-faire* approach, the writings of the American Studies movement seemed a godsend: a movement trying to offer a confederation of courses which would serve to reveal the interrelations between the studies of different aspects of American life.

Notes

1 *Humaniorautgreiinga: Humanistisk forsking i Noreg, del II [The Humanities Report: Humanist Research in Norway, Part II]* (Oslo: Rådet for humanistisk forsking [The Council for Research in the Humanities], NAVF, 1985), p. 12.

2
A Native Model: Culture Studies as an American Studies Discipline

American Studies as an interdisciplinary or multidisciplinary venture may be viewed as a return to the general cultural orientation that had traditionally characterized a humanist education. The emergence of the American Studies concept in the 1930s and 40s marked a growing dissatisfaction at American universities with the high degree of specialization within some established departments, in particular those of English and History. Tired of the sharp departmental barriers in the humanities, scholars wanted to expand the boundaries of their own research and teaching. In the 1950s the idea of American Studies found a stronghold in the departments of English, not least because of an increasing uneasiness with the hegemony of the New Criticism. By its insistence on the interrelations and interdependence of cultural phenomena, American Studies seemed to offer a way out from the New Critical prison-house of formalism.[1]

The classical manifesto of the emerging American Studies movement may be said to be Tremaine McDowell's *American Studies* from 1948. According to McDowell, American Studies was symptomatic of a general movement "away from extreme academic specialization toward a synthesis of knowledge." American Studies, McDowell declared,

> is the intellectual process whereby a student assimilates the complicated and often contradictory details of American civilization which he meets in his courses in social science, history, literature, philosophy, and the fine arts. And it is the intellectual process whereby he fashions out of them a picture of these United States. In so doing, he reduces diversity to some degree of unity.[2]

This seems wonderfully promising to native and non-native scholars alike, until they discover that McDowell's Whitmanesque celebration of the totality of American life does not really include any particular methodological suggestions or analytical illustrations of how this "intellectual process" of synthesizing different fields can be brought about.

The American Studies venture nevertheless expanded rapidly with the founding of the American Studies Association in 1951, the appearance of its official journal *American Quarterly*, and the introduction of American Studies programs at numerous colleges and universities during the 1950s and 60s. The publication of Henry Nash Smith's *Virgin Land: The American West as Symbol and Myth* in 1950 had given an important impetus to the concept of American Studies – a pioneer work attempting to relate ideas in both serious and popular literature to historical developments and dominant sociocultural ideas and values. In demonstrating the importance of symbols and myths as strategies for both literary *and* cultural expression, it came to be regarded as prototypical of what was later termed the "myth-and-symbol" school of American Studies, which was held to include, among others, such works as Leo Marx's *The Machine in the Garden* (1964) and Alan Trachtenberg's *Brooklyn Bridge: Fact and Symbol* (1965).[3]

The Myth-and-Symbol School

These myth-and-symbol works had a great impact not only in America but also abroad, above all in departments of English. They appealed to teachers of American literature who at the same time saw themselves as philologists with a general cultural orientation. At the same time they became important to "Background" teachers who were trying to study and teach the general characteristics of American culture. Concerned as they were with the interrelations of literature and culture, the teachers of English at foreign universities were attracted to the myth-and-symbol works for their promise of a genuinely interdisciplinary approach.

As my own work as an American "Background" teacher involved the study and teaching of everything from the class structure of the United States to its system of government and its foreign policy, however, the applicability of such a myth-and-symbol approach had its limitations as an interdisciplinary venture. If on the one hand the works of the myth-and-symbol school represented a reaction against the ahistorical literary criticism of the 1940s and 50s, they could on the other hand be argued to be colored by the aesthetics of the New Criticism, as Winfried Fluck suggests in an essay on American Studies;[4] in Smith's *Virgin Land,* Lewis's *The American Adam,* and Marx's *The Machine in the Garden,* culture as well as literature seems to be reduced to a dualistic conflict between ideas like innocence vs. corruption, embodied in such dualistic metaphors as the prelapsarian vs. the fallen Adam, or the garden vs. the machine. What may be lost in this kind of analysis is the sense in which culture represents an interplay of quite complex belief patterns that reflect a heterogeneous, diversified social experience. As Thomas A. Krueger puts it: "The histories of the Edenic Myth exhibit a suprisingly weak feeling for the texture of American life: its differentiations of class, religion, and ethnicity; its distinctive regional variations; its generational divisions; and the basic distinction between the sexes."[5] And, although I do not agree with all of the objections to the myth-and-symbol studies raised in Bruce Kuklick's well-known essay from 1972, I believe he touches upon a related point concerning cultural analysis when he says that "the imputation of collective beliefs is an extraordinarily complex empirical procedure," and that American Studies humanists have been all too eager to speak of "'the popular conception of American life,'" "'the American view of life,'" and the like.[6]

In addition, the theoretical discussion of myth and symbol in several of these American Studies works is awkward in the sense that myths and symbols are sometimes conceptualized as being mythofictional and sometimes as being sociocultural. In this manner, they become strangely subjective yet collective notions floating about in a no-man's land between illusion and reality. In his Preface to the first edition of *Virgin Land*, Smith speaks of myths as "an intellectual construction," and as "products of the imagination" existing "on a different plane" from empirical fact.[7] This emphasis on myth as a "mental construct," a term used also by Leo Marx in an essay on American Studies,[8] establishes a dualism between myth and sociocultural experience that is detrimental to a genuinely cultural analysis. Of course cultural myths may not function as accurate representations of the sociohistorical state of affairs at a specific time; this, however, makes them no less a part of those affairs. Culture can be said to be precisely the result of the interplay between social circumstances and the meanings that people impose on them, a point also conceded by Smith in his 1970 preface to *Virgin Land*.[9]

The theoretical shortcomings of the myth-and-symbol works prevent them from serving as models either for a methodical study of American culture or for a systematic cultural interpretation of American literature. Indeed, already towards the end of the 1950s and subsequently in the 60s, the American Studies interdisciplinary venture met with doubts as to its feasibility and practicability. McDowell's idea of synthesis, of trying to see American society as a whole, was an aim to which most American Studies scholars subscribed. The problem, however, was that it proved to be an ideal difficult to realize in practice. Perhaps because of the high hopes raised by the vision of some all-embracing interdisciplinary approach, many scholars within American Studies started to voice their disillusionment with the program.

Multidisciplinary vs. Interdisciplinary American Studies

It was actually Henry Nash Smith who had opened the discussion in 1957 with his essay "Can 'American Studies' Develop a Method?" He suggested that one unifying method had so far failed to appear, and that American Studies at this stage would have to content itself with being "a collaboration among men working from within existing academic disciplines but attempting to widen the boundaries imposed by conventional methods of inquiry."[10] Other scholars pointed out that even the collaboration between teachers from different disciplines was very problematic, and that neither the teachers themselves nor the students were able to evolve a truly synthetic perspective.[11]

In 1960, Robert E. Spiller cautioned against demanding some total unity of literary and historical studies, as it might end with a divorce between literature and history and thus bring defeat to the entire enterprise of American Studies.[12] Symptomatic of the state of American Studies at this time is Marshall W. Fishwick's statement in his introduction to a collection of essays from 1964 called *American Studies in Transition* that "No ready-made solution or method for our subject is in sight," and his hope that "the range and diversity of material will provide the impact that other fields derive from a unity which we have neither claimed nor sought."[13] In an essay from 1968 entitled "American Studies: Bird in Hand?", Fishwick ends with many questions concerning theory and method – and provides no answers.[14]

These were issues and doubts very similar to those I was struggling with in my own "Background" course in the mid and late 1970s in Norway, trying to forge some sort of synthesis between topics ranging from the checks and balances in American political institutions to the significance of country-and-western music. It was difficult indeed to find some shared cognitive objectives for the study of these various subject matters. And how could Americanists abroad hope to evolve a systematic interdisciplinary position when American Studies scholars in the United States felt unable to do so?

There is a strange contradiction between this sober assessment of the state of affairs of American Studies at this time both in the United States and abroad, and the fact that American Studies periodicals, American Studies associations, and American Studies university programs grew in number throughout the 1960s and early 70s. Periodicals like the *American Quarterly, American Studies,* the British *Journal of American Studies,* the *Canadian Journal of American Studies, American Studies in Scandinavia,* and *American Studies News* all testify to this development. By 1972, for example, there were at least 200 American Studies programs in operation in the United States, of which 153 offered bachelor's degrees, 24 master's degrees, and 29 doctoral degrees.[15]

The expansion becomes less than impressive, however, when one takes a closer look at most of these programs. On a 6-week trip to the Unied States during the summer of 1975, which included visits to several major universities in the East, the South, and on the West Coast for the express purpose of looking into their American Studies programs, I found that the great majority of these programs reflected considerable vagueness and uncertainty of planning, purpose, and aims.[16] The programs were often loose combinations of courses offered through different departments. Sometimes (in rare cases) a couple of courses were taught jointly by two or three teachers from different departments (usually the departments of English and history, with the occasional addition of political science or sociology). Thus the great majority of the universities had American Studies "programs," not departments; when a given number of topical courses was reached, one qualified for a degree or a minor in American Studies. Thus American Studies programs often reflected what Jay Mechling, Robert Merideth, and David Wilson in 1973 called the "Do-It-Yourself-Synthesizer-Kit-Fallacy" which

> not only encourages students to take whatever they wish from various disciplines. . . but directs them to put it all together – as in the spastic chant: two, four, six, eight – integrate! . . . the task of synthesis, the study of culture, is dumped on the novice student, as if he with his uncorrupted, natural talents were better suited to the hardest imaginable intellectual work than those who ought to know better.[17]

Similar critiques of the current state of affairs in American Studies made the movement suffer its most serious crisis to date during the late 1960s and early 70s. Misgivings and forebodings of failure were also intensified by a similar disillusionment with attempts at integration in other closely related fields.

The attacks were directed at two major theoretical pillars of the American Studies structure, namely the concept of interdisciplinary synthesis and the idea of cultural holism. The failure of interdisciplinary integration was noticeable even between the study of literature and the study of history or social science. Henry Nash Smith had suggested already in his 1957 essay that the two areas had so far proved incompatible because the literary critic tends to "cut aesthetic values loose from social fact," and the social scientist "uses techniques of research which make it difficult or impossible for him to deal with the states of consciousness embodied in serious art."[18]

This state of affairs had its parallel in the field of history where there was, or so it seemed, an unbridgeable gap between the intellectual historians of the 1950s and early 60s and the new social and economic historians of the late 60s and 70s. These new historians concentrated on smaller community studies rather than the nation as a whole, and they concerned themselves with empirically and statistically verifiable information rather than with the interpretation of some general American character or "mind."[19] There was also a growing interest in a specifically behavioral or sociological rather than a cultural approach to the study of history.[20]

The works of the myth-and-symbol school, as well as the historical studies of the 1950s and 60s, were especially criticized for being too consensus-oriented, emphasizing unity rather than conflict in their interpretation of American life. In one sense, this is somewhat unfair vis-à-vis studies like Smith's *Virgin Land* and Marx's *The Machine in the Garden*, which both dealt directly with cultural contradictions and conflict. Along with a great many of the intellectual histories at this time, however, they lean towards a holistic perspective repudiated by the new historians, to whom American life seemed fundamentally heterogeneous and diversified, even fragmented and disjoined. In the studies of the United States published in the 1970s, there was an increasing emphasis on pluralism and disunity, which seemed to discredit the search in American Studies for some synthetic approach to the analysis of American life.

These tendencies notwithstanding, the idea of an integrated, holistic-oriented discipline has persisted unabatedly to the present time. Since the 1970s there have consequently been two main trends in American Studies, one multidisciplinary and pluralistic, the other interdisciplinary and synthetic. Each has its obvious dangers and pitfalls. The synthetic approach may, for example, lead to a disregard of cultural differences between and within various social groups, and the multidisciplinary approach may, for example, result in a disregard of the ideological homogenity in the United States, the conformity to basic political and economic assumptions across class and ethnic lines, which is so striking as well as so surprising to the foreign student of American life.

What the early holistic works of American Studies nonetheless did was to analyze the myths and symbols around which hegemonic belief patterns of American life were organized (in the 19th and early 20th centuries in particular). Thus, the myth-and-symbol school was dealing with something that the multidisciplinarians subsequently ignored – the function of collectively held world views. Often implicit in the multi-disciplinarian approach to American Studies is the normative view that ideological hegemony is to be resisted, that cultural pluralism should be respected, and that the humanist ideal ought to be communal variety rather than homogeneity, and openness rather than closure. Ultimately, however, such pluralist views are not irreconcilable with a holistic orientation. It is quite possible to combine a critique of hegemony with an understanding of its pervasive cultural function.

The recognition of differences – the perception of culture as a field of competing persuasions – may be complemented by an awareness of the fact that the impact even of alternative and oppositional views is dependent on the extent to which they can cross subcultural boundaries and become more widely – collectively – shared. There is no reason why the idea of pluralism should not be supplemented by the concept of collectivity.

Part of the attractiveness of pluralistic and multidisciplinarian approaches to American Studies is their assumption that the strength of the field is to be found in its openness and diversity. McDowell suggested already in 1948 that "when and if American Studies become departmentalized, they [note the plural term] will have lost one of the major reasons for their existence."[21] In a recent essay, David Nye sees American Studies as "a crossroads where many disciplines meet rather than a territory staked out and protected by methodological boundaries." Thus, pluralism is its strength; it is an "anti-discipline" of "many simultaneous discourses": "Searching for no single method, it will not embrace single interpretations."[22] In this type of multidisciplinary venture, one ranges freely across disciplinary studies and adopts whatever insights seem relevant for one's own research topic.

In terms of this view, American Studies becomes not so much a discipline as an area study, whose objective is simply to engender new modes and ideas for the understanding of American life. But these inroads and viewpoints, however interesting in their own right, may often turn out to have little or nothing to do with the understanding and use of language. The scholar of English as a foreign language, however, is per definition concerned with those shared conventions of language use that make communication possible. As these collective conventions are cultural as well as grammatical, the student of English must give precedence to an explicitly cultural approach to the study of American life.

Towards an American *Culture* Studies

It so happens that the concept of culture is precisely what the interdisciplinarians in American Studies have tended to focus on as a possible theoretical foundation for the integrated analysis of American civilization. The first central step in this direction was taken by Richard E. Sykes in an essay entitled "American Studies and the Concept of Culture: A Theory and a Method" (1963). Although Sykes emphasized that the student of American civilization should be introduced to the ideas and approaches of the humanities as well as the social sciences, he suggested that American Studies was to be primarily "the study of American culture. Culture is the key concept, the unifying concept, the root word which suggests both theory and method."[23] Sykes's suggestion has been followed up by other scholars dissatisfied with the theoretical confusions of traditional "interdepartmental" American Studies. A good example is the article by Jay Mechling, Robert Merideth, and David Wilson, "American Culture Studies: The Discipline and the Curriculum," published a decade after Sykes's essay:

> As we see it, the culture concept belongs at the center of an American Studies disciplinary matrix. The necessary if not sufficient condition for engaging in American Studies is an applicable theoretical model of culture in the largest sense, embracing elements ranging from the biological heritage through institutions and belief systems to individual phenomenal experience. The concept locates the terms of our activities as scholars and teachers. If the "transition to maturity" in American Studies is to be rich in ideas, exciting in debate and efficient in focus, it is to the concept of culture that attention should be paid.[24]

Although multidisciplinary studies will always serve as a major source of ideas and insights for American Studies scholars, the idea of culture may provide this enormous field with an interdisciplinary hub from which its various topical spokes spread out, and to which they lead back.

Theoretical discussions in Norway within the study of English as a foreign language have by no means been as comprehensive as the one referred to in the United States, but the debate in British Studies and American Studies has proceeded along similar multidisciplinary/interdisciplinary lines. One of the first characterizations of a multidisciplinary studies perspective is found in Sigmund Skard's *American Studies in Europe* (1958):

> The term "American" Studies in this book means the study of the Civilization, past and present, of the United States of America, principally the study of those aspects that are fundamental to all national civilizations: human and cultural geography, political, economic, social, religious, and intellectual developments, law and institutions, language, literature, and the arts.[25]

The multidisciplinary pursuit of American or British civilization, thus defined, is perhaps still the dominant one in the study of English in Norway,[26] but a more explicitly interdisciplinary cultural perspective is also being pursued.[27] At the end of the 1970s the designation of the field was changed from the somewhat odious "Background" to the more informative term "Civilization." Although "Civilization" certainly signals a more general, scientific approach to the study of American and British life, its diffuseness still fails to give the discipline any definite cognitive and theoretical focus. The official *Norwegian* designation, however, is *kulturkunnskap,* which in my opinion is a far better term; its equivalent in English would be (American and British) *culture studies.*

In my own research and teaching over the last decade or so, I have become convinced that the anthropological concept of culture provides the most systematic and productive foundation for the study of American and British life in the English department of a foreign university. It offers a shared scientific framework for the general interpretation of many different aspects of experience – be they regional, social, ethnic, political, economic, or religious. Most significant of all, as culture and language are inextricably interrelated and interdependent, a cultural approach to American and British Studies may be directly related to the study of language. In addition, the everyday cultural life of a nation may be linked to so-called "high" or "élite" culture; this invites the possibility of integrating a humanities and a social science perspective. The study of *culture* is therefore uniquely suited to demonstrate the close interconnections between language, literature, and society – which is, after all, the main objective of a foreign language study like that of English.

In this manner, my own search for a theoretical focus for the teaching and study of American life has followed a route parallel to the one signalled in the title of an essay by Gene Wise, "From '*American* Studies' to 'American *Culture* Studies.'"[28] As indicated by the emphases in Wise's title, this reflects a movement away from the conception of an American exceptionalism to the general study of cultural life. The study of American or British culture is not per definition a search for unique features; it is a systematic means of analyzing those that are typical.

It is by no means sufficient, however, to proclaim the importance of the concept of culture for an interdisciplinary approach to British or American Studies. If the term is to be of value for systematic scholarly research, it must be carefully defined. The next chapter will consequently present and discuss a definition that may serve as the foundation for culture studies within the study of English as a foreign language.

Notes

1. For the history of the American Studies movement, see for example Tremaine McDowell, *American Studies* (Minneapolis: Univ. of Minnesota Press, 1948); Robert H. Walker, *American Studies in the United States: A Survey of College Programs* (Baton Rouge: Louisiana State Univ. Press, 1958); Robert E. Spiller, "Value and Method in American Studies," *The Third Dimension: Studies of Literary History* (New York: Macmillan, 1965), pp. 199-216; Robert Merideth, ed., "Introduction: Theory, Method and American Studies," *American Studies: Essays on Theory and Method* (Columbus, Ohio: Charles E. Merrill, 1968), pp. v-xiv; Robert Sklar, "The Problem of an American Studies 'Philosophy': A Bibliography of New Directions," *American Quarterly*, 27 (1975), 245-262; Luther Luedtke, "Not So Common Ground: Controversies in Contemporary American Studies," in Luedtke, ed., *The Study of American Culture: Contemporary Conflicts* (DeLand, Fla.: Everett/Edwards, 1977), pp. 323-367; Gene Wise, "'Paradigm Dramas' in American Studies: A Cultural and Institutional History of the Movement," *American Quarterly*, 31, No. 3 (1979), 293-337; Guenther H. Lenz, "American Studies – Beyond the Crisis?: Recent Redefinitions and the Meaning of Theory, History, and Practical Criticism," *Prospects*, 7 (New York: Burt Franklin, 1982), 53-113; David E. Nye, "American Studies as a Set of Discourses," *American Studies in Scandinavia*, 17, No. 2 (1985), 51-63; and Giles Gunn, "American Studies as Cultural Criticism," *The Culture of Criticism and the Criticism of Culture* (New York: Oxford Univ. Press, 1987), pp. 147-172. As far as the history of American Studies abroad is concerned, see for instance Sigmund Skard, *American Studies in Europe: Their History and Present Organization* (Philadelphia: Univ. of Pennsylvania Press, 1958); and Robert H. Walker, ed., *American Studies Abroad* (Westport, Conn.: Greenwood Press, 1975).
2. McDowell, *American Studies*, p. 33 (see note 1, first item listed).
3. Smith, *Virgin Land* (Cambridge: Harvard Univ. Press, 1950); Marx, *The Machine in the Garden* (New York: Oxford Univ. Press, 1964); and Trachtenberg, *Brooklyn Bridge* (New York: Oxford Univ. Press, 1965). Often included among the "myth and symbol" works is John William Ward's historical study *Andrew Jackson: Symbol for an Age* (New York: Oxford Univ. Press, 1953); and R.W.B. Lewis's literary-oriented *The American Adam* (Chicago: Univ. of Chicago Press, 1955).
4. Fluck, "Aesthetic Premises in American Studies," in Robin W. Winks, ed., *Other Voices, Other Views: An International Collection of Essays from the Bicentennial* (Westport, Conn.: Greenwood Press, 1978), pp. 21-30.
5. Kreuger, "The Historians and the Edenic Myth: A Critique," *Canadian Review of American Studies*, 4 (Spring 1973), 8.
6. Kuklick, "Myth and Symbol in American Studies," *American Quarterly*, 24 (October 1972), 445.
7. Smith, *Virgin Land*, p. xi (see note 3).
8. Marx, "American Studies – A Defense of an Unscientific Method," *New Literary History*, 1 (1969), 86.
9. Smith, *Virgin Land*, p. viii.
10. Smith, "Can 'American Studies' Develop a Method?" in Joseph J. Kwiat and Mary C. Turpie, eds., *Studies in American Culture: Dominant Ideas and Images* (Minneapolis: Univ. of Minnesota Press, 1960), p. 14 – a revised version of his essay in *American Quarterly*, 9 (Summer 1957), 197-208.
11. See for instance Roy Harvey Pearce, "American Studies as a Discipline" and Edwin H. Cady, "'American Studies' in the Doldrums: Or Whistling Up a Breeze," both in Robert Merideth, ed., *American Studies: Essays on Theory and Method* (Columbus, Ohio: Charles E. Merrill, 1968), pp. 15-16 and 34-36. See also Robert Spiller, "Value and Method in American Studies," pp. 205-209 (see note 1, third item).
12. Spiller, "Value and Method in American Studies" (cf. note 1, third item) – a revised version of an essay entitled "American Studies, Past, Present, and Future," in Kwiat

and Turpie, eds., *Studies in American Culture*, pp. 207-220. Interesting in this connection is also the preface to a collection of essays entitled *American Perspectives* (1961), where the editors Robert E. Spiller and Eric Larrabee deplore that the volume did not achieve the unity they had hoped for.
13 Fishwick, ed., *American Studies in Transition* (Boston: Houghton Mifflin, 1969), pp. 7 and 9; first published by Univ. of Pennsylvania Press, 1964.
14 Fishwick, p. 340. This essay was first published in *International Educational and Cultural Exchange* (Department of State, Washington D.C., Winter 1968).
15 Cf. Jay Mechling, Robert Merideth, and David Wilson, "American Culture Studies: The Discipline and the Curriculum," *American Quarterly*, 25 (October 1973), 363.
16 I am grateful to the University of Tromsø for the grant that made this study tour possible.
17 Mechling, Merideth, and Wilson, 372 (see note 15).
18 Smith, "Can 'American Studies' Develop a Method?" p. 10 (see note 10).
19 For assessments of the field of American intellectual history, see for instance John Higham, "American Intellectual History: A Critical Appraisal" and Rush Welter, "The History of Ideas in America: An Essay in Redefinition," both in Robert Merideth, ed., *American Studies: Essays on Theory and Method*, pp. 218-235 and 236-253 (see note 11); Warren I. Susman, "History and the American Intellectual: Uses of a Usable Past," *American Quarterly*, 16 (1964), 243-263; John Higham, "Hanging Together: Divergent Unities in American History," *Journal of American History*, 61 (June 1974), 5-28; Gene Wise, "The Contemporary Crisis in Intellectual History Studies," *Clio*, 5 (1975), 55-71; and Robert Berkhofer, "Clio and the Culture Concept: Some Impressions of a Changing Relationship in American Historiography," *Social Science Quarterly*, 53 (1972), 297-320. For a series of re-examinations, see John Higham and Paul K. Conkin, eds., *New Directions in American Intellectual History* (Baltimore: Johns Hopkins Univ. Press, 1979).
20 See for instance Robert F. Berkhofer, *A Behavioral Approach to Historical Analysis* (New York: Free Press, 1969).
21 McDowell, p. 31 (see note 1, first item).
22 David E. Nye, "American Studies as a Set of Discourses," *American Studies in Scandinavia*, 17, No. 2 (1985), 51, 53, and 61.
23 Sykes, "American Studies and the Concept of Culture." *American Quarterly*, 15 (Summer 1963), 254. See also an essay by Gertrude Jaeger and Philip Selznick from 1964, "A Normative Theory of Culture," in Robert Merideth, ed., *American Studies*, pp. 93-123 (see note 11).
24 Mechling, Merideth, and Wilson, "American Culture Studies." 368 (see note 15).
25 Skard, *American Studies in Europe: Their History and Present Organization*, vol. 1 (Philadelphia: Univ. of Pennsylvania Press, 1958), p. 8.
26 For a multidisciplinary "Studies" view, see for example Dorothy Burton Skårdal, "Kulturkunskapens plass i engelskfaget" (Norwegian title but English text), *Språk og språkundervisning*, 12, No. 3 (1979), 46-54; Ragnhild Nessheim, "På vei mot en definisjon av kulturkunnskap som grunnfagsdisiplin?" *Språk og språkundervisning*, 15, No. 4 (1982), 27-30; and John Oakland, "British Civilisation: Institutions, Units and Problems at Grunnfag Level," in John Oakland, ed., "Working Papers in Civilisation Topics and Research," vol. 1 (Univ. of Trondheim: English Institute, 1984), last essay, pp. 1-9. Oakland's volume includes, among others, the two articles referred to above. Oakland has edited two additional volumes of "Working Papers in Civilization Topics and Research," vol. 2 (1985) and vol. 3 (1986), but most of the articles here deal with specific subjects rather than questions of theory and didactics.
27 For an interdisciplinary, synthetic approach, see Fredrik Chr. Brøgger, "For å kommunisere må man forstå andres tenkesett: Kulturkunskapen i engelskundervisningen i den videregående skolen," *Språk og språkundervisning*, 12, No. 4 (1979), particularly 40-42; and his "A Cultural Approach to American Studies," *American Studies in Scandinavia*, 12 (1980), 1-15. For an interesting interdisciplinary humanist approach combining literary study with cultural history and the history of ideas, see Øyvind Gulliksen, "Kulturkunnskapens plass i engelskfaget," *Språk og*

språkundervisning, 11, No. 4 (1978), 56-69. See also Annabelle Despard, "On the Teaching of British Civilization," *Språk og språkundervisning,* 17, No. 1 (1984), 47-58; and her "Multi-Cultural Education – A Special Need for All," in John Oakland, ed., "Working Papers in Civilization Topics and Research," vol. 2, pp. 49-72 (see end of note 26). Perhaps the most important Norwegian discussion to date of culture studies within foreign-language study is *Kulturkunnskap som forskningsfag* (Oslo: Rådet for humanistisk forskning, NAVF, 1988; see particularly the essays by Stein Haugom Olsen, "Kulturkunnskap som åndsvitenskap" and Jostein Børtnes, "Filologi og studiet av fremmedspråkenes kultur," pp. 25-34 and 46-56 respectively. For an interdisciplinary approach combining historical study and textual analysis, see Fredrik Chr. Brøgger, "Grinding the Gears of Production and Consumption: Representational versus Nonrepresentational Advertising for Automobiles in the Mid-1920s," *Prospects,* 15 (1990), 197-224.

28 Wise, "From 'American' Studies' to 'American *Culture* Studies': A Dialogue Across Generations," *Prospects,* 8 (New York: Cambridge Univ. Press, 1983), 1-10.

3
The Study of Dominant Assumptions and values: Culture Studies as an Anthropological Discipline

Culture is a notoriously imprecise term, used in widely different contexts in the social sciences as well as in the humanitites. Even in anthropology itself there seem to be nearly as many definitions of culture as there are anthropologists. In a monograph from 1952 entitled *Culture: A Critical Review of Concepts and Definitions,* A.L. Kroeber and Klyde Kluckhohn discuss more than one hundred and sixty definitions of the term.[1] One of the most common points of departure for modern anthropology seems to be Edward B. Tylor's definition from 1871 of civilization or culture as "that complex whole which includes knowledge, belief, art, morals, law, custom and any other capabilities and habits acquired by man as a member of society."[2] This concept of culture is all-embracing, however, and includes the behavioral ("customs"), the creative-material ("art"), the normative and institutional ("morals" and "law"), and the cognitive ("knowledge" and "belief") – not to mention "any other capabilities and habits." Such an inclusive definition may be appropriate for a field like "civilization," amorphously conceived, but it does not provide any specific cognitive focus for a concept of culture that may link it to the study of language and thus to the teaching of English.

The following discussion should therefore not be regarded as a treatise on how anthropology should define its own culture concept – obviously that is for anthropologists and ethnographers to decide, not scholars of English. Instead, the purpose here is to examine anthropological definitions of culture in order to discuss the ones most relevant for language-oriented analysis. Some anthropologists, less all-embracing than Tylor, define culture so as to make it signify actual behavior, others so as to make it represent material artifacts and products, and yet others so as to make it designate people's view of the world. Whereas many Anglo-American definitions in the first half of this century tended to conceive of culture as empirically observable features such as habits, customs, and artifacts, quite a few post-World War II definitions see it in terms of the ideas and values shared by the members of a society or a social group. It is this latter definition that seems most auspicious for the study of language, because linguistic proficiency is also a matter of familiarity with commonly held assumptions encoded in ordinary discourse.

Culture Conceived as Belief Systems

The concept of culture defined as people's world view is also the one most closely related to the traditional concerns of the humanities. In the humanities, *culture* has been an élitist and aesthetic concept involving, as Matthew Arnold put it, the best which has been thought and said in the world. Thus, the study of ideas has been central to the humanities as well – but primarily in terms of the interpretation of individual works of, for example, literature, philosophy, or the arts. The anthropological concept of culture, however, is a non-élitist and collective one, designating the belief systems held by people in general. Culture in this anthropological sense represents the habitual discourse of assumptions and norms that most people, through upbringing and socialization, adopt and share. Both the élitist-aesthetic and the collective concepts of culture are important for language study. Whereas the study of a literary work, however, ultimately deals with the issue of how its language gives expression to a *particular* vision of the world, the cultural study of an ordinary conversation or text ultimately deals with how its language gives expression to a *general* discourse of collective beliefs and values. With such a viewpoint we have arrived, it seems to me, at the very *raison d'être* for culture studies within the study of a foreign language.

It may be useful for further discussion to look at some definitions of culture along these lines. In an essay entitled "The Concept of Culture" (1945), for example, the anthropologists Clyde Kluckhohn and William H. Kelly define it as "those historically created designs for living . . . which exist at any given time as potential guides for the behavior of men."[3] In a joint essay from 1958, "The Concepts of Culture and of Social System," the anthropologist A.L. Kroeber and the sociologist Talcott Parsons suggest that culture refers to "transmitted and created content and patterns of values, ideas, and other symbolic-meaningful systems as factors in the shaping of human behavior and the artifacts produced through behavior."[4] And Clifford Geertz, to take one last example, presents the following condensed definition (1957): "Culture is the fabric of meaning in terms of which human beings interpret their experience and guide their action."[5] According to all these definitions, the study of culture involves the analysis of a collective "fabric of meaning" that defines people's way of life.

One important aspect of these definitions is that they all focus on the interrelationship between behavior and values. The concern with behavior indicates that people's belief systems are not meant to represent some general "mind" or "spirit of the age" so often evoked in the humanitites. Instead, culture is seen as the meaning that may be attributed to people's verbal and non-verbal conduct in social life. Cultural studies thus proceed from the same concrete phenomena as do sociological studies. It is the cognitive objectives of these studies that are different; whereas sociological studies are concerned with the ways in which specific social relations operate, the study of culture concerns itself with the ideational implications of such relations. Although culture according to this conception is *abstract,* it is no less real than the concrete phenomena of which it serves as the ideological expression. As Kroeber and Kluckhohn so succinctly put it, "Analytical abstractions summarize an order of relationship between natural phenomena, and relations are as real as things."[6]

This accentuation of *relationship* may, like the definitions above, help us to avoid getting caught in the materialist vs. cognitive controversy in present-day anthropological theory. Culture may be seen as neither behavior as such nor ideas in themselves, but as a semiotic system expressing the relationship between them. Cultural assumptions do not exist apart from behavior, and behavior cannot be considered apart from cultural assumptions. Like the everyday stories and symbols that embody them, cultural beliefs and values must be seen as behavioral strategies, as much part of the public domain as any actual event. The suggestion that cultural assumptions "guide" or "govern" behavior, for example the use of language, is therefore not an assertion of the primacy of ideas *vis-à-vis* social relations. Instead, it may be read as the expression of their interconnectedness; ideas and behavior signify each other. The conception of cultural beliefs *guiding* conduct also serves to emphasize their non-deterministic function *vis-à-vis* behavior. The word "guide," however, could be exchanged with the term "determine" if the concept of determination is defined, as Raymond Williams suggests in his book *Marxism and Literature,* as "setting bounds" and "exerting pressures,"[7] which may be precisely the way in which culture patterns function in social life.

Conceptions of Culture: Unity vs. Diversity

This function of belief systems in "setting bounds" is related to another central aspect of each and all of the definitions above, namely the issue of cultural coherence. Kluckhohn and Kelly speak of culture as "designs" for living, Kroeber and Parsons of "content and patterns," and Geertz of a "fabric of meaning." Similar phrases alluding to the way in which cultural assumptions constitute a whole are found among many cultural anthropologists, who use additional terms like "configurations," "structures," "systems," "webs," or, to quote Geertz adding to this imagistic profusion, "a set of control mechanisms – plans, recipes, rules, instructions (what computer engineers call 'programs') – for the governing of behavior."[8] Such formulations may indicate that culture is seen as a totality tied together by various webs or patterns of beliefs and values. Obviously such holistic conceptions of culture were also behind some of the "consensus" works of American intellectual history and American Studies during the 1950s and 60s. This trend towards holistic interpretation fell into disrepute in the aftermath of the racial, ethnic, sexual, and sociopolitical confrontations of the American 1960s, which engendered changes not only in society at large, but within the academic institutions as well. Series of new curricula were introduced, such as Black Studies, Native American Studies, and Women Studies.[9] As Gene Wise has put it, these developments

> imposed massive strain on the old intellectual history synthesis. After the middle of the sixties, it was hard to assume without question that America is an integrated whole; division and conflict, not consensus, seemed to characterize the culture. It was also difficult to assume the privileged position of élite ideas as a window into the culture. . . . Intellectually, American Studies has never recovered from the earthquake-like jolts of the sixties, and the consciousness those events forced upon the culture.[10]

Seeing culture as a sort of "fabric" of meanings, however, is not synonymous with regarding it as a totality unified by a few basic premises. It is quite possible to emphasize cultural complexity and conflict and still accentuate the interconnections between particular cultural ideas and between belief systems. By defining *culture* as *patterns* of ideas and values we can have it both ways. The indefinite plural suggests that culture is pluralistic and variegated, while the word itself implies that some beliefs are patterned, interrelated with each other.

In this manner it may be suggested that culture is partially characterized by "a strain toward consistency"[11] or "a tendency toward internal coherence."[12] There is, for example, a marked strain-toward-consistency concept in Gunnar Myrdal's well-known work on American blacks, *An American Dilemma* (1944), where the United States is described as having, of all the countries of Western civilization, "the *most explicitly expressed* system of general ideals in reference to human interrelations."[13] According to Myrdal, this "American Creed" (embodying values such as liberty and equality) caused a mental uneasiness in the white majority, a cultural guilt that would be resolved when American blacks joined the mainstream of American economic, political, and social life. Other passages, however, show that Myrdal's vision of a culture straining towards consistency was qualified by a more conflict-oriented conception as well:

> The moral struggle goes on within people and not only between them. As people's valuations are conflicting, behavior normally becomes a moral compromise. There are no homogeneous "attitudes" behind human behavior but a mesh of struggling inclinations, interests, and ideals, some held conscious and some suppressed for long intervals but all active in bending behavior in their direction.[14]

A far more radical conception of cultural diversity is found for example in Victor Turner's *Dramas, Fields and Metaphors,* where "the culture of any society" is said to be "more like the debris, or 'fall-out,' of past ideological systems, than it is itself a system, a coherent whole."[15]

By defining *culture* as *patterns* of assumptions and values rather than as *a* (i.e. *one*) *system* of such patterns, we avoid having to take sides in this holism-vs.-debris debate. Such a definition gives us the opportunity to regard a culture as embodying dominant and oppositional patterns of beliefs, which may mutually confirm as well as conflict with each other.[16] It should also be emphasized that cultural discord is not only found between dominant and oppositional ideologies, but also between, and within, dominant belief systems themselves. A case in point is the contradictions in American mainstream culture between the belief in free enterprise, the faith in big business, and the idea of equal opportunity; another is the conflict between a production and a consumption ideology, involving ideas of industry vs. gratification, of self-denial vs. self-indulgence. Even within deeply held core values there are radical discrepancies. Often the cultural "fabric of meaning" is frayed and stretched to the limit; the dominant "patterns of ideas" may be seen as much a matter of discord and contradiction as of harmony and unity.

Although American Studies scholars are, as Gene Wise observes, "less inclined now to take readings from a single vantage point on *The American Experience*" and instead regard America "from a variety of different, often competing, perspectives,"[17] a major distortion would be produced if such competing perspectives were discussed without taking account of their relative importance and influence. Some cultural beliefs in a society are after all "more equal than others." Representing the values of prestigious social groups and power élites, some culture patterns play a dominant role. Thus, culture patterns should also be analyzed and discussed in relation to the social and economic relations of which they are part. The idea of dominant culture traits may be linked to Marxist concepts such as superstructure, ideology, and hegemony, which have all been used also to refer to prevalent beliefs and values that serve to legitimize the power of the ruling class. For example, taking off from Antonio Gramsci's discussion of *hegemony* as a continual process of class domination and subordination, Raymond Williams characterizes it as

> a central system of practices, meanings and values, which we can properly call dominant and effective . . . a whole body of practices and expectations; our assignments of energy, our ordinary understanding of the nature of man and of his world. It is a set of meanings and values, which as they are experienced as practices appear as reciprocally confirming. It thus constitutes a sense of reality for most people in the society, a sense of absolute because experienced reality beyond which it is very difficult for most members of the society to move, in most areas of their lives.[18]

This conception of hegemony comes very close to the idea of *dominant culture patterns* used in this study.

The degree of identification with the prevalent culture will of course vary from social group to social group. Certain groups that see themselves as living on the periphery of, or in opposition to, mainstream society may disregard or reject dominant ideas outright. Even in such cases, however, their reactions are defined by the culture they defy. And most other groups tend to share many of the most fundamental assumptions and values of the socio-economic system of which they are part.

The more a student of culture emphasizes the importance of factors such as class dominance and the mode of production for the formation of culture, the more his/her culture concept will be related to Marxist concepts like ideology, superstructure, and hegemony. Most students of culture, however – whether Marxists or non-Marxists – would agree that economic factors play a basic role in the formation of culture. In most cases, too, they would speak of a complex interrelationship between economic base and cultural superstructure. It would take a very simplistic student of culture and a very "vulgar" Marxist to talk about a direct, one-to-one relationship between economic conditions and culture patterns, and not grant the development of cultural institutions – whether those of law or those of art – some degree of intrinsic autonomy. Although they would emphasize that society and ideology are dialectically related, students of culture would nonetheless in many cases tend to agree with the sense of priority inherent in Marx's suggestion that "It is not the consciousness of men that determines their existence, but, on the contrary, their social existence determines their consciousness."[19]

The conception of *dominant* culture patterns may also be related to the much-abused idea of national character. In an essay from 1966, for example, Jules Henry defines *national character* as "*a group of interrelated motivations, values and feelings prevailing among a people;*"[20] this is not unlike the conception of culture as mainstream beliefs and values programming people's behavior. The term "character" tends, however, to carry too many holistic connotations and needs to be qualified by the idea that "a" people – even in the hegemonic sense – holds a mesh of competing and conflicting cultural assumptions and motivations. It would also be important to emphasize that the study of national character would involve the analysis of what is typical rather than what is necessarily unique. "National character" is in part an "international character" as well: several dominant culture patterns in the United States are for example cross-cultural ones too and shared with Britain and other Western European cultures – for example those patterns connected with free enterprise and bourgeois liberalism. With these reservations, however, the definition of national character as dominant culture patterns may serve to rescue the term from its ill repute as a static or ethnocentric concept; instead of being associated with cultural homogeneity, it becomes resituated within the context of cultural variety and continuous historical change.[21]

Much of the cultural knowledge we hold as members of society is often, as John L. Caughey suggests, "tacit rather than explicit; we operate with it, but it is not on the surface of awareness and we cannot articulate it fully."[22] Social scientists speak, with slightly different emphases in each case, of for example "explicit" and "implicit" culture patterns,[23] or "overt" and "covert" ones,[24] or "avowed" and "masked" ones.[25] Without caring to draw too fine distinctions here, this study will term those patterns *explicit* that are openly expressed and sanctioned, and those patterns *implicit* that are immanent either because they are unreflected upon or because they are repressed. Some dominant cultural ideas may, for example, be such an ingrained part of the social context of everyday life that they remain unconscious; they may be so habitual, so much a matter of course, that they appear "natural" – seem part of the nature of things. Repressed features, however, may represent emerging patterns of anxiety and dissatisfaction which conflict with more publicly sanctioned culture traits. Whatever their type, implicit culture patterns can often be disclosed in texts only by way of close analysis.

Definition of the Discipline of Culture Studies

The preceding discussion of the concept of culture may be extensive enough to provide us with an exemplary definition to be used within the study of English as a foreign language. Thus I propose that *culture studies* be defined as *the study of mutually confirmative and conflicting patterns of dominant assumptions and values signified, explicitly or implicitly, by the behavior of members of a social group and by the organization of their institutions.* The final point also connecting culture patterns to people's institutions is in one way superfluous; institutions, whether political or cultural ones, are also products and representations of behavior. The subject of institutions is nevertheless explicitly mentioned because the political ones in particular have traditionally featured prominently in the syllabuses of the study of English. The central point in the definition above, however, is that the examination of how such (or other) institutions are organized is not the final aim of culture studies; the final step in the analysis would focus on the basic assumptions and values inherent in the ways in which the institutional system operates.

This culture concept consequently provides us with a particular focus for our investigation of American or British life. Instead of the presentation of mere historical, sociological, and political facts and figures, which used to characterize the study of "Background," such knowledge is now only a means to an end, namely the imputation of dominant belief systems. This objective is far more relevant to the study of language than providing only socio-economic and political information. Whether our subjects are government, class conflicts, religious denominations, or the system of education, the ultimate aim of our analysis is their ideological implications. It is important to emphasize, however, that culture as such is not static. Social and cultural changes are interdependent; thus, culture must be conceptualized not as some passively held philosophy, but as the signification of behavior – as the collectively shared strategies by which people deal with their everyday situations and make sense of their own existence.

The definition above springs, however, partly from the American Culture Studies debate and partly from my own particular interests as a foreign language scholar. Definitions used in British Culture Studies are sometimes – like those of the Birmingham Centre for Contemporary Cultural Studies – more directly grounded in economic conditions and class struggle issues. One such example is Richard Johnson's Marxian characterization of the subject of culture studies as *"the historical forms of consciousness or subjectivity."*[26] There is, however, no radical discrepancy between such a conception of culture and the definition provided above; it is a matter of emphasis.

One of the main advantages of my somewhat elaborate definition is to be found in the flexibility of the term "social group." On the one hand, it may be stretched so as to refer to the nation as a whole and designate some of its dominant culture patterns; on the other hand, it may refer to a particular group of people within the nation and designate the culture patterns of that specific group. This makes it possible to discuss, on the one hand, patterns of dominant ideas and values that typify American life in a particular period, and to describe, on the other hand, what is for example characteristically Chicano about the life of Mexican Americans in the same period. Such a culture concept therefore makes room for discussing the variations in culture patterns among social groups according to region, class, ethnicity, religion, race, gender, and so on. At its best, such a culture study may provide an intellectual conception of what it means, at a specific time, to be an American, or a Southern American, or a working-class American, or an Afro-American, or an American woman – or say, a black American middle-class woman.

Such a definition may lend itself directly to anthropological research. Indeed some of the recent work of American Studies scholars has involved the ethnographic study of contemporary American subcultures.[27] Of course, it would also be possible for a Scandinavian scholar of American Culture Studies to spend a year, say, in San Francisco or a small Midwestern town and observe life there, keeping a day-to-day diary, finding and establishing contact with particular informants, interviewing them, researching local archives, visiting local museums and community centers, studying objects of material culture, witnessing religious practices, recording political events, and so on and so forth. But this kind of research cannot be the main objective of culture studies within the field of foreign language study. The anthropological concept of culture gives the discipline its cognitive focus – that of the analysis of dominant assumptions and values – but the methodology will be very different from the fieldwork involved in traditional ethnography, partly because foreign language students are often barred from firsthand acquaintance with the culture, and partly because of the overriding concern in language departments with textual-linguistic material for study and research.

Foreign language subjects lend themselves easily to the study of written texts, where the interplay between culture and language can be analyzed closely and systematically. Thus, although the concept of culture stakes out the cognitive direction for the work within British and American Culture Studies, it must be combined with the close analysis of how cultural ideas and values are imbedded in the very language of a text. The analytical process by which we identify dominant assumptions in texts is not unlike the method by which we arrive at the central themes of a literary work. Some social scientists like James Spradley use, in fact, the term *"cultural theme"* for "assertions that have a high degree of generality" in a culture.[28] The use of the term "theme" for "dominant assumptions" serves to illustrate that the analytical activities of humanities scholars and social scientists are often more closely related than they themselves tend to think.

Interpreting a text from a linguistic-cultural point of view, however, involves paying close attention to its its grammatical constructions, its choice of register, its idiomatic nuances, its web of semantic interconnections, its use of imagery, etc. The field of culture studies is thus per definition interdisciplinary, a synthesis of cultural and linguistic analyses of written sources. These sources may be taken from different areas of life, express the views of various social groups, and represent different types of text – be they oral interviews, personal diaries, weekly magazines, newspaper reports, advertisements, political speeches, Supreme Court decisions or, say, country club rules and regulations.

A Culture Studies Analysis of a Text

Let me examine the text of an advertisment as an illustration of a culture studies analysis as I have attempted to define it in this chapter. It is an advertisement for a perfume called "Aromatics Elexir," which belongs to a series of cosmetic products trademarked "Clinique."[29] It is not clear from the advertisement at which social group it is directed, beyond the fact that the product is explicitly said to be for women. As is the case with much advertising, it may be assumed that it is directed at a large, undefined middle-class audience. And the text indeed reflects some of the ideas of success that play a dominant role in American middle-class ideology:

Non-Conformist.

For good reasons, all of Clinique is fragrance-free. Then why is a perfume sold at Clinique counters?

It started out as a service. For customers who wanted a fragrance that typified the unique qualities of the Clinique woman.

Aromatics Elexir was the answer. But for years, Clinique let it be a private discovery, and didn't say much about it. Quietly left it on its own, to sink or swim.

Aromatics Elexir was noticed. Asked about. Words spread that this blend of herbs and essences has remarkably magnetic effects. It performs. Attracts interest. Gets fascinating results.

Find it only at Clinique counters. Spray it on. See for yourself why it's like no other perfume.

Aromatics Elexir never conformed. Needed no fanfare. It's the only self-made perfume success.

The language used to present this perfume gives expression to two quite different culture patterns of success in American life. One has to do with the belief in individualism and being self-made, and the other with the idea of personality and making success through one's appeal to *others* (by using a product or selling oneself or both). The phrases of the second, third, and last paragraph evoke the first-mentioned idea of "self-made... success"; the perfume is connected with "unique qualities," a product which was "left on its own," "to sink or swim." The headline and the last paragraph connect this uniqueness with the idea of being "Non-Conformist," an ultimate compliment that evokes both behavioral and intellectual independence. Of course, the advertisement allegedly presents the success of the product, not the woman using it. At the same time, however, the attributes of the product are identified with the those of the woman, as its fragrance is said to typify "the unique qualities of the Clinique woman." By way of the advertisement's own analogy, then, the person buying the product is also connected with individual autonomy and nonconformity. In this manner the perfume is made desirable in terms of the deeply cherished ideals of self-reliance in American culture, calling to mind somebody who, in the sociologist David Riesman's term, is "inner-directed," following her or his own values and convictions.[30]

In the fourth paragraph, however, we discover that this success story has primarily turned into a matter of "being noticed." The idea of success seems at this point to be linked with public performance – with the ability to "perform" and have "magnetic effects." Here again, the attributes of the product become part of the woman wearing it as well. When the "blend of herbs and essences" is said to get "fascinating results," the distinction between the product and its user has become quite blurred (a blend may "produce" "effects," whereas "getting results" would tend to imply some human agent). This second version of successfulness makes it into a matter of popularity, where the individual succeeds not by way of self-reliant competitiveness, but by way of social skills. The language used here thus calls to mind the type of person whom David Riesman calls "other-directed" and William Whyte terms *The Organization Man* – somebody who courts the favor of others within a corporate-hierarchical structure.[31] The importance of having an appealing personality and personal magnetism has been proclaimed in hosts of modern success manuals, for example in the writings of Dale Carnegie and Norman Vincent Peale. As Willy Loman puts it in Miller's *Death of a Salesman,* "the man who creates personal interest, is the man who gets ahead. Be liked and you will never want"; "...that's the wonder, the wonder of this country, that a man can end with diamonds here on the basis of being liked!"[32] What is evoked in the second part of this advertisement, then, is the 20th century vision of success as a matter of personal attractiveness.

Grammatically speaking, the very syntax of this text may itself be said to signify – to function as a formal representation of – some of the ideas discussed above, particularly the idea of activeness and the concept of attracting attention. The text constantly makes use of incomplete sentences, most often without grammatical subjects. The result is a clipped, terse style of clauses reduced to pure verbal action, as in "Aromatics Elexir was noticed. Asked about," or "It performs. Attracts interest. Gets fascinating results." If one transforms the latter sequence into one sentence: "It performs, attracts interest, and gets fascinating results," we see that it becomes explanatory and discursive, whereas the original gives us a sense of hammering in a series of effects. The thematic prominence syntactically given to the verbs here creates a sense of activity and movement very appropriate for the idea of achieving success. In addition, the way in which this use of language breaks with the conventions of ordinary discursive prose makes it, indeed, become "noticed" and attract "interest." This is an important point in the second success version of this text: success as a matter of style.

In sum, the text gives expression to two dominant myths of success in American life: first the culture pattern of individualism stressing values like nonconformity, "sink-or-swim" competitiveness, and self-made success, and then a culture pattern of personality-oriented values emphasizing magnetism, attractiveness, and popularity. Reflecting two different visions of the world, those of entrepreneurial vs. corporate capitalism, these culture patterns involve such dichotomies as self-reliance vs. self-promotion, and character vs. personality.

Of course the text, by identifying the product with both culture patterns, suggests that they are mutually *confirmative*. By viewing self-made success as a product of a unique attractiveness, the text tries to have its cake and eat it too. At the same time, however, it discloses, inadvertently as it were, the ideological ruptures in the very mediation that it has tried to create. First of all, there is the intrinsic inconsistency in the text itself: if the "Clinique woman" typifies the same "unique qualities" as the product, she surely would have little need for a perfume producing "magnetic effects" *for* her. What the advertisement actually suggests, of course, is that, as so few of us come equipped with a self-made drive and a fascinating personality, we need something instead that can provide us with the necessary exceptional attributes. Thus, the text may be said to contain an *explicit* message, that of self-reliance and singular performance, and an *implicit* one, that of the end of self-made individualism, of the need to turn to consumer products in order to make ourselves special, which reflects an other-directed dependence not only on people, but on goods.

This textual contradiction is accentuated by a *contextual* one as well; although the advertisement celebrates the idea of a perfume succeeding on its own – by word of mouth, so to speak – the very fact that it is now being advertised casts doubt on the adequacy, in this day and age, of something being self-made, of something remaining "a private discovery." Implicitly, the advertisement proves that large-scale advertising is indeed necessary in a mass society in order to achieve maximum profit. (In addition, it is of course caught up in the inherent contradiction of all advertisements selling products in terms of the concept of singularity: if the ad succeeds on a mass scale, the users of the product would inevitably cease to be unique.)

The contradictions inherent in the advertisement thus typify important ideological conflicts in contemporary American life. Of course, this cultural split between inner-directedness and other-directedness is found in most Western societies; it is an international trend as well. It may be argued, however, that this schism is more acute and irksome in the United States than in most other countries because of the extreme adherence in America to the competitive values of free enterprise. Cherishing the ideal of self-made individualism, Americans are at the same time extensively committed to a consumption ideology of personal appearance and passive gratification, according to which mass consumer products themselves may provide the individual with the exceptional attributes that she or he desires.

The discussion of this advertisement – disclosing its implicit as well as its explicit culture patterns – is merely one illustration of the kind of analysis of texts that in my opinion must be the central concern of culture studies as a humanities discipline. Such textual analysis, however, requires some familiarity with linguistics as well as discourse analysis – with what the next chapter terms a "cultural linguistics."

Notes

1 Kroeber and Kluckhohn, *Culture: A Critical Review of Concepts and Definitions* (New York: Vintage Books, 1963; originally published 1952 as vol. 47, no. 1 of the Papers of the Peabody Museum of American Archeology and Ethnology, Harvard University).
2 Tylor, *Primitive Culture,* vol. 1 (London: John Murray, 1920; originally published 1871), p. 1.
3 Kluckhohn and Kelly, "The Concept of Culture," in Ralph Linton, ed., *The Science of Man in the World Crisis* (New York: Columbia Univ. Press, 1945), p. 97.
4 Kroeber and Parsons, "The Concepts of Culture and of Social System," *American Sociological Review*, 23 (1958), 583.
5 Geertz, "Ritual and Social Change: A Javanese Example," *The Interpretation of Cultures* (New York: Basic Books, 1973), p. 145.

6 Kroeber and Kluckhohn, *Culture*, p. 375 (see note 1).
7 Williams, *Marxism and Literature* (Oxford: Oxford Univ. Press, 1977), pp. 84, 87.
8 Geertz, "The Impact of the Concept of Culture on the Concept of Man," *The Interpretation of Cultures*, p. 44 (see note 5).
9 For a discussion of these new tendencies, see for example Robert Sklar, "The Problem of an American Studies 'Philosophy': A Bibliography of New Directions," *American Quarterly*, 27 (August 1975), 245-262.
10 Wise, "'Paradigm Dramas' in American Studies: A Cultural and Institutional History of the Movement," *American Quarterly*, 31, No. 3 (1979), 314. For discussion of the issue of uniformity vs. diversity, see also Jay Mechling, "If They Can Build a Square Tomato: Notes Toward a Holistic Approach to Regional Studies," *Prospects*, 4 (New York: Burt Franklin, 1979), pp. 61, 64-67.
11 Cora DuBois, "The Dominant Value Profile of American Culture," *American Anthropologist*, 57 (1955), 1232-1233.
12 Philip Bock, *Modern Cultural Anthropology: An Introduction* (New York: Knopf, 1969), p. 310.
13 Myrdal, *An American Dilemma* (New York: Harper and Row, 1962; originally published 1944), p. 3.
14 Myrdal, p. lxxii.
15 Turner, *Dramas, Fields and Metaphors* (Ithaca: Cornell Univ. Press, 1974), p. 14.
16 See for example Raymond Williams, "Base and Superstructure in Marxist Cultural Theory," *New Left Review*, 82 (November-December 1973), 10.
17 Wise, "'Paradigm Dramas' in American Studies," 319 (see note 10).
18 Williams, 9 (see note 16).
19 Marx, "Preface to *A Contribution to the Critique of Political Economy*," in Lewis S. Feuer, ed., *Marx and Engels, Basic Writings on Politics and Philosophy* (London: Fontana, 1969), p. 84.
20 Henry, "A Theory for an Anthropological Analysis of American Culture," in Joseph G. Jorgensen and Marcello Truzzi, eds., *Anthropology and American Life* (Englewood Cliffs, N.J.: Prentice-Hall, 1974), p. 9.
21 For a more extensive analysis of the problems involved in the study of national character, see Walter P. Metzger, "Generalizations about National Character: An Analytical Essay," in Robert Merideth, ed., *American Studies: Essays on Theory and Method* (Columbus, Ohio: Charles E. Merrill, 1968), pp. 145-173; and Alex Inkeles and Daniel J. Levinson, "National Character: The Study of Modal Personality and Sociocultural Systems," in Gardner Lindzey and Elliot Aronson, eds., *The Handbook of Social Psychology*, vol. IV (Reading, Mass.: Addison-Wesley, 1969), pp. 418-506.
22 Caughey, "Ethnography, Introspection, and Reflexive Culture Studies," *Prospects*, 7 (1982), 117.
23 Consult the definition of Kluckhohn and Kelly cited earlier and the discussion on pp. 99-102 of their essay "The Concept of Culture" (see note 3).
24 See Bernard Bowron, Leo Marx, and Arnold Rose, "Literature and Covert Culture," in Joseph J. Kwiat and Mary C. Turpie, eds., *Studies in American Culture: Dominant Ideas and Images* (Minneapolis: Univ. of Minnesota Press, 1960), 84-95, particularly pp. 84-87.
25 See Richard E. Sykes, "American Studies and the Concept of Culture: A Theory and a Method," *American Quarterly*, 15 (Summer 1963), pp. 257-260.
26 Johnson, "The Story So Far: And Further Transformations?" in David Punter, ed., *Introduction to Contemporary Cultural Studies* (London: Longman, 1986), p. 280.
27 See for example Jay Mechling, "If They Can Build a Square Tomato: Notes Toward a Holistic Approach to Regional Studies," *Prospects*, 4 (New York: Burt Franklin, 1979), 59-77. An important influence from ethnography has been the work of James Spradley, for example *The Cultural Experience: Ethnography in a Complex Society* (1972, co-authored with David McCurdy) and *You Owe Yourself a Drunk: An Ethnography of Urban Nomads* (New York: Little, Brown, 1979).
28 James P. Spradley, *Participant Observation* (New York: Holt, Rinehart and Winston, 1980), pp. 140, 141.

29 Clinique advertisement from *Cosmopolitan,* 199, No. 6 (December 1985), 23.
30 See Riesman, with Nathan Glazer and Reuel Denney, *The Lonely Crowd: A Study of the Changing American Character* (Garden City, N.Y.: Doubleday, 1953).
31 See Whyte, *The Organization Man* (Harmondsworth: Penguin, 1963; originally published 1956).
32 Arthur Miller, *Death of a Salesman* (Harmondsworth: Penguin, 1961), pp. 25-26; 68.

4
Culture and Language: Culture Studies as a Linguistics Discipline

Some 20 years ago, language studies within the field of English in Norway were seldom carried beyond the unit of the the single sentence. The dominance of structuralist approaches in linguistics made teachers and students ignore, and even deny, the importance of sociocultural context for the understanding and acquisition of language. English was studied for its general structural laws which, once they were grasped and acquired, were thought to ensure the necessary linguistic competence. Once one learned the distinctive features and "rules" of phonology and grammar, one would be able to understand and use the English language correctly. This was, in short, a linguistics that never went beyond the study of the formal properties of language – that dealt almost exclusively with the Saussurean *la langue* rather than *le parole*, with the Chomskyan *competence* rather than *performance*, with *language* rather than *speech*.[1]

As far as the discipline of semantics was concerned, it would be unfair to say that it was left out of the study of the English language, but it too was pursued at this time primarily in terms of the construction of general laws of meaning, which were abstracted from, and hence regarded as independent of, the actual sociocultural contexts in which the language was being used. The study of semantics focused on highly generalized rather than discourse-specific classifications of meaning.

Certainly no one can dispute the overriding priority of a general grammatical competence for the acquisition of a foreign language. Moreover, as long as linguistic analysis was limited to the study of the single sentence, questions of a non-formal nature were easily precluded. The non-contextual, isolated sentence was, of course, an intellectual construction by linguists alone; no one comes across such an entity in real life. This type of approach, however, engendered a gulf between the study of linguistics and the study of culture. The field of literature seemed to be in an intermediate position; all camps paid lip service to its importance for language study, but in practice linguists and literary scholars dealt with the study of language in ways so different that no one could actually believe that they were complementary.

Contextual Linguistic Theories

Over the last two decades, however, the discipline of linguistics has been systematically carried far beyond the formal study of the individual sentence. In particular, developments within the fields of *functional linguistics, sociolinguistics, pragmatics,* and *disccourse analysis* have opened up possibilities for a *rapprochement* between the studies of language and culture. Common to these fields is the concern with language *use,* with seeing language as acts of communication between a speaker/writer and a listener/reader. The majority of linguists today would acknowledge the importance of *context* for the study of communication. The following statement by Stanley Fish, a literary critic influenced by speech act theorists, could stand as a basic presupposition of these contemporary schools of linguistics: "A sentence is never not in a context. We are never not in a situation. A statute is never not read in the light of some purpose. A set of interpretive assumptions is always in force. A sentence that seems to need no interpretation is already the product of one."[2] The study of this extra-grammatical context of the assumptions and intentions involved in human discourse is now deemed necessary for a more comprehensive understanding of the way in which language functions. Any student of language must, as Roger Fowler puts it, answer the question of "'Why this sentence? Why have all the other possible sentences been rejected?' It is obvious that grammar in itself, the individual's ability to produce English, or French, or Russian, sentences, gives no reason at all for the production of one sentence rather than another. ."[3] Non-formalist linguistic approaches therefore attempt to explain how context helps to produce particular phrases, sentences, and utterances.

Fields like functional linguistics, pragmatics, sociolinguistics, and discourse analysis all deal with various types of contextual issues. It is not the objective here, however, to give a comprehensive presentation of these disciplines in order to give a survey of the multiple ways in which different extra-linguistic factors may be seen to determine language use. This chapter has the more limited aim of trying to demonstrate the interdependence of language and *cultural* context, to analyze some of the ways in which specific language uses are produced by, and reflect, particular dominant assumptions and values – particular ideological strategies – in a society.

This specific concern with the cultural aspects of communication consequently makes for a much more narrow focus than, for example, that of a functional grammar, which for instance in M.A.K. Halliday's work involves the comprehensive study of the various ideational, interpersonal, and textual functions of language use.[4] A predominantly cultural objective would also preclude the extensive concern in sociolinguistics with the study of the varieties of language according to class, region, ethnicity, and so on.[5] Some of these differences do not necessarily reflect different cultural strategies; the difference, say, between the British "I have got" and the American "I have gotten" is merely a geographical one, and having or not having a so-called post-vocalic /r/ in America may merely indicate a difference in region/class. At the same time, however, the use of particular pronunciations and grammatical constructions from dialects, sociolects, or registers of speech may *in particular contexts* assume a specific cultural function. They may be used to express identification with specific subcultures and particular ideological points of view. In some cases, too, syntactic, lexical, and stylistic usages may, for example, serve as means of social control – a way in which élite groups may underscore their authority and assert their power.[6] To the extent that sociolinguistics as well as functional linguistics in this manner lead to a concern with the interrelations between language and ideology, they are of course directly relevant to cultural analysis.

As far as pragmatics is concerned, our exclusive concern with cultural context precludes large parts of its comprehensive mapping of the general principles and maxims that govern the situational production of speech acts. Language philosophers like J.L. Austin and J.R. Searle as well as a great many linguists tend to discuss these conversational "rules" as if they constitute a general functional system analogous to the structural one of grammatical "correctness."[7] The result is that speech act maxims and appropriateness conditions are seldom related to specific cultural issues. In pragmatics, therefore, there is a need for research focusing on the ways in which different types of speech acts may assume culture-specific functions. To the extent that various kinds of illocutionary and perlocutionary acts also represent sociocultural strategies and goals in a given situation, they are of course of great interest for a study of the interdependence of language and culture.

Whereas both sociolinguistics and pragmatics have evolved as distinct subdisciplines within linguistics, the status of discourse analysis is more vague. Discourse is sometimes defined so inclusively as to refer both to the general cultural context of language use and to the more specific situational contexts for speech act production, as well as to the intrinsic context of significations constructed by the language within a particular speech or text itself. In this chapter, discourse analysis will be limited to the latter phenomenon – the study of "the use of sentences in combination," as H.G. Widdowson puts it.[8] Whenever sentences are strung together – be they those of a dialogue, a speech, or a text – their language serves in itself to construct a particular kind of cohesion and coherence, an intrinsic context of formal and semantic structures, which helps to determine their message. Again, however, these structures are of interest for a cultural study only insofar as their production serves to express certain dominant patterns of beliefs and values.

In conclusion, then, we may say that neither sociolinguistic, functionalist, pragmatic, nor discourse-oriented aspects of language use are necessarily culturally significant. It is only when they can be shown to have a specific ideological signification and function that they become objects of study for the field that I would term *cultural linguistics*. Such cultural linguistics may be defined as the study of the ways in which patterns of dominant assumptions and values are the product of certain language uses, and vice versa. The sociolinguist William Labov has in fact suggested that a so-called *speech community* may be defined not so much "by any marked agreement in the use of language elements . . . as by participation in a set of shared norms."[9] It is the various sets of shared norms that must serve as the central focus for a cultural approach to language.

Towards a Cultural Syntactics and Morphology

As an analytical approach, cultural linguistics requires an extensive understanding of the structures and functions not only of the language, but also the beliefs and values, of a particular society. As Roger Fowler puts it, "a 'sufficiently rich' theory of linguistic performance demands not merely a cataloguing of the types of sentences that occur in texts but also a powerfully explanatory model of the culture (or relevant parts of it) which makes texts the way they are."[10] Relatively little work has been done within linguistics in this respect, partly, I suspect, because a concern with culture would make for a far more relative and interpretive science than the study of the "rules" of, say, morphology, syntax, and philosophical pragmatics; linguistics would thus be carried a considerable step away from the logical and hard-science stringency which it traditionally has sought to emulate.

Like all context-oriented linguistic disciplines, a cultural approach to the study of language rejects the radical distinction in structuralist thought between language as a formal system on the one hand, and the specific uses to which language can be put on the other. The *choice* of certain formal structures cannot be kept distinct from the sociocultural designs that they are made to serve. Thus we may speak of a *cultural syntactics,* a *cultural morphology,* and a *cultural semantics* as well as a *cultural pragmatics* and a *cultural discourse analysis* – each of which will be treated in the following discussion.

The most controversial of these subdisciplines are those of a cultural syntactics and morphology – to suggest that particular types of grammatical contructions may be chosen to express particular cultural strategies and assumptions. However, language use must be understood, as M.A.K. Halliday puts it, by "looking at what the speaker says against the background of what he might have said but did not, as an actual in the *environment* of a potential. Hence the environment is defined paradigmatically: using language means making choices in the environment of other choices." In Halliday's view, any text must thus be regarded "as an actualized potential; which means that you have got to study the potential."[11] This holds true for choices not only of lexicon but of grammatical structures. If there has been, say, a demonstration in the United States in which feminists and right-to-lifers have clashed (and where neither party could be clearly blamed for having initiated the confrontation), this may be reported as "Feminists clash with right-to-lifers" or as "Right-to-lifers clash with feminists." As "clash" merely designates a conflict between two or more parties, the actual choice of word order – of grammatical subject and object in the sentence – inevitably reflects an ideological position; the choice of subject is at the same time a designation of agent. More "neutral" constructions like "Feminists and right-to-lifers clash" or, more abstractly, "Abortion issue triggers clash," do not escape being normative, either; they are ideologically significant precisely because causality and agency are obscured or omitted.

To choose a grammatical construction is consequently not an innocent activity. If we look for instance at the word order of more than one adjective qualifying a noun, we discover that the adjectives that are felt to be more objectively classificatory ones are placed closest to the noun, whereas more subjectively descriptive adjectives are placed at a further remove from it. Their word order is thus sometimes an index of basic cultural assumptions and valuations. In American or British English, for example, one would normally say "a black female doctor" and not "a female black doctor," because sex qualification is – in grammatical-ideological terms, as it were – felt to take precedence over color-qualification. Still, the expression "a female black doctor" is certainly possible, and *could* in a specific context reflect a racist attitude because of its reversal of the more common word order.[12] (The semantic fact that one also chooses to be sex- or color-specific about doctors *could,* of course, in itself be an ideological sign of sexism or racism.)

The syntax of a sentence thus inevitably designates a way of ordering the world in specific ways. Words paratactically combined with one another in the same syntactic constituent will, for example, assume a common function *vis-à-vis* other sentence constituents. Thus, in the sentence "The goverment will ensure self-determination and independence for individuals, businesses, and local communities," the persons, companies, and communities of the object complement will inevitably appear to have the same relationship to "self-determination and independence." Words are not merely a combination of signs referring "out" to our experience; the way in which words are syntactically arranged also helps to constitute that experience. It is thus the *grammatical* juxtaposition of the noun phrases in the sentence above that helps to create the ideological impression that individuals, businesses, and communities would need or want the same type of autonomy and freedom. Thus, the syntax itself contributes to the *construction* of a conservative bourgeois vision which glosses over the possible conflicts of interest between workers, employers, and society.

A similar example is the following statement in President Ronald Reagan's State of the Union Address from January 25, 1984 : "We're seeing rededication to bedrock values of faith, family, work, neighborhood, peace and freedom – values that help bring us together as one people, from the youngest child to the most senior citizen."[13] Even without the additional modification of the last relative clause, the very fact that "faith, family, work, neighborhood, peace and freedom" are brought together as a post-modifier to "values" makes them – grammatically, so to speak – appear to be something more than an enumeration of various discrete items in the world "out there"; they automatically appear to have a unity, an interconnectedness, indicative of a specific ideological way of viewing the world. (This is indeed what Reagan himself suggests later in the speech when he returns to these words and declares: "For us, faith, work, family, neighborhood, freedom, and peace are not just words; they're expressions of what America means . . ."[14]).

It is not my intention to suggest that certain types of syntactic construction necessarily have, *in themselves,* certain ideological implications. What I do argue, however, is that grammar in practice always assumes a particular realization, and that particular uses of grammar, in particular contexts, always reflect certain intentions, goals, and purposes, which in some cases are culturally significant indeed. Moreover, such grammatical usages can certainly be systematically analyzed. Let me illustrate this further by looking closely at the following two passages from President Ronald Reagan's 1984 State of the Union Address:

> As we came to the decade of the eighties we faced the worst crisis in our postwar history. The seventies were years of rising problems and falling confidence. There was a feeling government had grown beyond the consent of the governed. Families felt helpless in the face of mounting inflation and the indignity of taxes that reduced reward for hard work, thrift, and risk-taking. All this was overlaid by an ever-growing web of rules and regulations.

It's time to move forward again, time for America to take freedom's next step. Let us unite tonight behind four great goals to keep America free, secure, and at peace in the eighties together.

We can ensure steady economic growth. We can develop America's next frontier. We can strengthen our traditional values. And we can build a meaningful peace . . . [15]

Syntactically speaking, these two passages are worlds apart. In the second passage, where Reagan presents the goals of his own administration, the sentence constructions follow the basic, unmarked pattern of English, with **S + V + O** (subject plus verb plus object): *We can ensure . . . growth, We can develop America's . . . frontier, We can strengthen our . . . values, And we can build . . . peace.* In all these cases, the verbs are transitive, and the voice is without exception active. The syntax itself communicates simplicity, directness, and action, which are also semantically accentuated by the choice of the personal pronoun "we" (the subject for the verbal process is thus a human agent), as well as by the connotations of movement in words like "growth," "develop," and "build."

"Unmarked pattern" is in a way a misleading phrase for these particular syntactic constructions: they stand out not merely as being transitive, but as being what Gunther Kress and Robert Hodge call *transactive.* In their *Language as Ideology,* Kress and Hodge operate with a theory of two basic semantic-syntagmatic models, *relationals* and *actionals,* in which the latter are subdivided into *transactives* and *non-transactives.* A transactive sentence model designates an "action passing on from an actor to an affected"[16]; in a non-transactive model, the actor or the affected is left out. Reagan's declarations all take the form of transactives. It is the consistent use in these sentences of a transitive as well as transactive *grammar* that in itself helps to portray Reagan's free enterprise ideology as action-directed, dynamic, and object-oriented. Syntax and semantics go hand in hand in these examples.

In the first passage, however, the grammar itself serves to bring across a quite different message. With the exception of the first sentence (and one subordinate instance later in the paragraph), the clauses are all intensive or intransitive, and the majority of them are relational. In addition, one sentence is in the passive voice, and another serves as a kind of masked passive construction. The second sentence is, for example, merely relational: *The seventies were years of . . .* The noun phrases *years of rising problems and falling confidence* are nominal transformations of intransitive constructions like *problems rose* and *confidence fell;* once "uncovered," these clause structures overtly demonstrate what the nominals in a way partly "hide," namely that any reference to an affected entity is deleted, and that the grammatical subjects represent mere abstractions which convey no sense of any human agents – no sense of particular policies by particular parties causing these "problems" to rise (for someone in particular).

By such types of *nominalization* transformations, complicated relations are, as Kress and Hodge put it, "collapsed into single entities," and "Simplicity can be asserted where in reality complexity is the case."[17] Discursive prose often abounds with such morphological/syntactic transformations. In other paragraphs of Reagan's speech, for example, we come across sentences like "we have . . . cut well over 300 million hours of *government-required paperwork* each year" (saving "the public more than $ 150 billion over the next 10 years"), and "To reduce the threat posed by *abandoned hazardous waste dumps*, EPA will spend $410 million . . ."[18] (my italics). A nominalization like *government-required paperwork* makes the actual process of government "cuts" into an abstraction where the people affected are conveniently deleted. A construction like *abandoned hazardous waste dumps* avoids identifying any actors making and dumping this "threat" as well as those who are affected by it. The result is not merely that of abstraction; as Kress and Hodge point out, by way of nominalizations of this kind, what was originally a process is transformed into a state, an "activity" is turned into "object," and something specific assumes the form of something general.[19] This is a way in which the choice of a certain type of *morphology* assumes a certain kind of ideological function, that of not only simplifying but obscuring and glossing over the particulars of social processes and actions.

To return, however, to the syntactic constructions of Reagan's first passage, the third sentence represents once more a relational rather than an actional sentence model, an "existential-*there*" construction: *There was a feeling government had grown beyond the consent of the governed.* This "feeling" thus becomes a sort of existential condition without reference – an absolute state. The subordinate clause *[that] government had grown beyond the consent of the governed* serves simply an intensive, non-transitive function; as subject, government is made to exist absolutely, which is indicated also by the use of zero article or pronoun. (There is no agent, it seems, which causes its growth; Reagan speaks in a preceding passage of "the tendency of government to grow, for practices and programs to become the nearest thing to eternal life we will ever see on this earth."[20])

The fourth sentence also represents a mere relational syntactic model: *Families felt helpless in the face of mounting inflation and the indignity of taxes* ["that reduced reward for hard work, thrift, and risk-taking"]. The verb "felt" is merely an intensive verb that links families with a condition, that of helplessness. The adverbial qualifying the verb phrase, *in the face of . . . inflation and . . . taxes,* once again reflects a use of nominals that creates a sense of a state rather than a process; such a sentence constituent appears even less process-oriented than the passive construction which it perhaps could be said to mask: *Families [were made] helpless [by] inflation and taxes.* The nominal construction *the indignity of taxes* makes revenue into a pure (and semantically negative) abstraction – a metaphor which suggests that taxes inherently cause indignity. This curious abstraction is part of the grammatical subject of a rare phenomenon in this passage, a transitive construction: *[inflation and the indignity of taxes] that reduced reward for hard work, thrift, and risk-taking.* The grammatical subject eradicates, however, any awareness of human agents.

In one form or another, vagueness of causality has been a syntactic characteristic of all of these sentences, but the fifth and concluding sentence represents the epitome of this sort of indeterminacy: *All this was overlaid by an ever-growing web of rules and regulations.* The passive construction may have been motivated by its linking function; the subject "all this" sums up something in the preceding statement(s), but what "all this" may refer to is impossible to determine. In a passive clause like *all this was overlaid by . . .* it may be pointed out that its construction with noun + "be" + participle bears a close resemblance to the construction of noun + "be" + adjective. The passive thus produces a sense of a finished process, a state rather than an action; this is also a result of the thematic prominence that the passive construction gives to the (grammatical) object of its active counterpart.[21] (The fact that the preterite *overlaid* in the active transformation *a web of rules overlaid all this* would be unusual in English, also serves to illustrate how irreversibly *passive* this particular passive construction is.)

The active construction *a web of rules overlaid all this* may nonetheless serve as a final illustration of the tendencies inherent in this passage as a whole, namely the use of grammatical subjects that are consistently non-human. Abstractions like "problems," "confidence," "government," "inflation," "taxes," and "web [of rules and regulations]" function (often in various transformed versions) as if they were agents, as if they performed actions, instead of being the result of them. This represents an obfuscation and mystification of the actual political processes and the agents and agencies involved. In this passage, then, Reagan's speech *syntactically* and *morphologically* presents the world of the 1970s as a mysterious universe whose only subjects and agents are impersonal and abstract. No wonder, therefore, that people are said to feel helpless; this is a *grammar,* so to speak, of alienation. The very syntax of these sentences helps give expression to the kind of anti-welfare state ideology that was dominant in American life and politics in the 1980s. Reagan's own free enterprise policies are expressed grammatically in transitive, transactive and object-producing terms, whereas the earlier ("non-productive") welfare state ideology is perceived in non-transitive, intransitive, and non-transactive terms. This is in itself a striking example of the function of a particular type of *cultural syntactics*.

This is not to say, however, that those who wrote this speech deliberately fashioned syntactical patterns like these. It was instead, I believe, the writers' ideology that made them, perhaps largely unconsciously, choose such a series of constructions. The main point, however, is that grammar and culture are inextricably related. Our students should be made aware not merely of the fact that choices of linguistic constructions represent different ways of saying things, but that they involve differences which make a difference. In their culture studies classes, they should be taught to understand and discern how particular grammatical constructions may function as signals and signs for particular cultural strategies and valuations. In order to do so, however, they must know something about the nature of language, on the one hand, and the nature of culture, on the other.

Towards a Cultural Pragmatics and Semantics

Grammar, narrowly defined, only gets us part of the way. In addition, for example, a type of *cultural pragmatics* is necessary – the study of how the speech acts of a given discourse assume culture-specific functions. A case in point is Reagan's tendency to open many of his televised speeches with "My fellow Americans." In formal terms, the function of this phrase is a *phatic* one, similar to a formula like "Ladies and gentlemen" – an act of communication which initiates a contact between speaker and listener. At the same time, however, the expression "my fellow Americans" has a specific cultural-semantic function, that of establishing the image of an everyman's President – on the one hand a king-like father-figure raised above petty interest-group politics, and on the other hand a man of the people, speaking directly and familiarly to each and all. (In addition, of course, there are the Christian connotations of being charitably disposed towards one's neighbor, one's fellow men.) The cultural function of this speech act is thus a many-faceted one – to project a democratic ideology which at the same time serves to gloss over the fact that the speaker, in this case President Reagan, actually represents particular interests and particular political policies. It would be misleading to suggest that the phatic-formulaic and the cultural functions of Reagan's expression are separate. For analytical purposes, they may be discussed separately, but the expediency of the phrase "my fellow Americans" consists precisely in the fact that it represents a "deep-structural" cultural strategy that masks itself as a mere "surface" formula.

Thus, in speech act analysis, one must look at both the formal-pragmatic and the cultural-pragmatic function of acts of communication. Two examples (among many) from Reagan's 1984 Address must suffice. One is his already quoted statement that "We're seeing rededication to bedrock values of faith, family, work, neighborhood, peace, and freedom ." The illocutionary act involved here is a so-called *representative,* that is, the act of stating that something is the case. Reagan simply asserts that Americans have once again become dedicated to certain individual-centered values. But to leave the pragmatic analysis here would be to ignore the strategy that this statement is made to serve in the context of the total communication situation for Reagan's speech – its function as an extended address from a particular speaker to a particular audience. It is important to keep in mind that Reagan's annual State of the Union Address is a policy statement to Congress, which in this particular case argued for, among other things, a reduction of taxes and federal spending as well as an increase of the defence budget. What Reagan is also doing, therefore, is to sell his own policies in terms of a representation of widely accepted American beliefs, as if these dominant beliefs and his particular policies policies were synonymous. Rhetorically speaking, he is not simply involved in the speech act of *(re)presenting* some American core values, he is also involved in the act of inviting his listeners to identify *his* policies with these generally accepted beliefs. This is a typical instance in which speech act analysis merges into, and must be combined with, discourse analysis.

A particularly interesting illustration of the necessity for such an analytical combination may be found in Reagan's assertion that "For a time we forgot the American dream is not one of making government bigger; it's keeping faith with the mighty spirit of free people under God."[22] Here are two representatives: asserting that the American Dream itself entails a delimitation of government growth, and asserting that the Dream is synonymous with freedom and religious devotion. When two such representations of the American Dream are combined as discourse, their parataxis makes the listener automatically assume that there is some sort of *coherence* between them – that reduction of federal spending is indeed a matter of freedom and, if one will, a belief in God. The point is that the explicit formulation of such an assertion would immediately have triggered a critical reaction. By being expressed in an implicit manner, in terms of speech acts of which each has a separate representative function, Reagan gets away with making his listeners identify his own fiscal policies with the American Dream itself, including the ideas of freedom and religion. In this sense, the formal-pragmatic and the cultural functions of discourse are again inseparable. In nearly all his public speeches, Reagan was a master of implicitly making people identify his specific political doctrines with a generally accepted ideology, thus obscuring the fact that his strategies, if and when enacted, would serve to benefit particular social groups and be detrimental for others.

The most basic and indispensable subdiscipline of what I have termed a cultural linguistics, however, is a *cultural semantics*. The fact is that, in many cases, students will only be helped part of the way when looking up words or word combinations in a dictionary. To quote the Danish-Norwegian author Axel Sandemose, "Every word is contaminated by every mouth through which it has gone, and that means quite a few as time passes, and then it has been written almost the same number of times and has not become less infected from that. . . . A word means a hundred different things more than a dictionary knows of."[23] Of course it cannot be an aim of foreign language teaching to make students aware of the nuances of words to the extent that native speakers are aware of them. An objective of culture studies must nevertheless be to acquaint the students with a *collectively shared* American and British cultural vocabulary which, for sociohistorical, economic, and political reasons, has come to play a dominant role in the definition of the world views of these societies. Such a cultural vocabulary can only evolve from a systematic study of culture, and the evolution of such a linguistic-cultural approach must have a high priority in culture studies.

Let me choose only one example (among many) from Reagan's 1984 State of the Union Address, which illustrates the necessity for a cultural semantics. Referring to the present (the 1980s), Reagan asserts that: "Americans were ready to make a new beginning, and together we have done it."[24] A *new beginning:* even a reader with little command of English would get the literal meaning of this phrase, but in addition he or she need to know something about the significance of words like "new" and "beginning" in the history of American culture: about the "new nation" of the Declaration of Independence; about a statement like "Four score and seven years ago our fathers brought forth on this continent, a new nation" (from the Gettysburg Address); about countless immigrants coming to America to make a "new beginning"; about Americans moving from the East to the West (or wherever) to make a "new" life for themselves; and so on and so forth. This ideology of *the new* in American history and culture has of course been politically appropriated by liberals and conservatives alike, in our own age for example by Roosevelt and his "New Deal" and by Kennedy and his "New Frontier," as well as by Reagan. The point is simply that without the *cultural semantics* that the field of culture studies provides, one would miss completely the central sociohistorical resonances of such phrases, sentences, and arguments.

It should perhaps be pointed out that few conservatives have been so clever as President Reagan in making use of this ideology of *the new,* more precisely in making highly conservative ideas appear new and revolutionary. A closer look at his two Presidential Inaugural Addresses as well as his Annual Addresses to Congress shows that they are shot through and through with this type of "old-as-new" synthetic vocabulary. This leads me to the last subject for discussion, that of a cultural approach to *discourse analysis.*

Towards a Cultural Discourse Analysis

The study of any speech act must also deal with the intrinsic semantic interplay of words, phrases, and sentences – with the question of how a dialogue, a text, or a speech *as a whole* makes culture-specific sense. This involves the kind of analysis of language in which, I might add, our students become very well trained through their close study of literary texts, and which is indispensable to any extended analysis of language use.

The cultural-semantic analysis of the ideology of *the new* in Reagan's 1984 State of the Union Address should consequently not be limited to the two isolated sentences discussed above. Because a text represents a particular use of language, it is also a manifestation of cultural ideas whose version is never quite the same from one text to another. Part of the analysis of textual discourse is therefore to study the intrinsic interplay of meanings in a text, by which it expresses an individualized version, as it were, of a sociocultural vision. The scope of this chapter does not allow any close and comprehensive analysis of the extended discourse of Reagan's 1984 Address, but it may be instructive to simply look at the way in which Reagan employs the "old/new" motif throughout his speech. The survey on top of next page presents some of the most striking examples of this (with italics added), excerpted from Reagan's speech and classified according to the ideology of "the new," the ideology of "the old," and an ambivalent or middle-ground position.[25]

When Reagan declares that America has a "new strength" and has undertaken "new methods," his "ideology of the new" seems quite definite and unqualified. This is part of his projection of an America "reaching for its future with confidence," as he puts it in a subsequent passage. This future orientation becomes a bit more ambiguous, however, when he for example compares the "new world" of space with the clipper-ship oceans of early and mid 19th century commerce; here "newness" inevitably also evokes a sense of repetition. The same is

The Ideology of the New	The Ambivalent/Middle Position	The Ideology of the Restoration of the Old
"America's *new* strength, confidence, and purpose are carrying hope ..."	"... America is much *improved* ..."	"America *is back* – standing tall ... "
"'Civilization *cannot go back* ... We have undertaken *new* methods.'" [Quote from Franklin D. Roosevelt]	"Americans were ready to make a *new beginning* ..."	"Hope is *reborn* for couples ..."
	"It's time to move *forward again*"	"We're seeing *rededication* to bedrock values ... "
"Our second great goal is to ... develop ... our next *frontier:* space."	"The *tide* of the future is a freedom *tide* ..."	"Congress ... helping us *restore* pride ... to our military."
"Just as the oceans opened up a *new world* for clipper ships ... space holds enormous potential ..."	"There was a hunger in the land for spiritual *revival;* if you will, a crusade for *renewal.*"	"But we must do more to *restore* discipline to schools ..."
	"After all our struggles to *restore* America, to *revive* confidence in our country, we can*not*, must *not* and will *not turn back.*"	"why can't freedom to acknowledge God be *enjoyed again ...*"

true of the characterization of space as "our next frontier," by which Reagan's "Star Wars" are conceptualized in terms of the 18th and 19th century conquest of the American continent. These ambiguities notwithstanding, the dominant semantic implications here are nevertheless those of dynamic progressiveness.

Other passages of Reagan's speech, however, express an explicit vision of the present-day restoration of the old. When Reagan speaks of "**re**dedication to bedrock values" and "hope . . . **re**born," he evokes a sense of recurrence at the same time. His express wish to "**re**store discipline to schools" and "**re**store pride" in America's military (capability) similarly evokes his desire to shape the world of the present in terms of the past. Reagan's conservative commitment to values of the past is also directly asserted in his declaration that America "is *back*" as well as in his desire to have school prayers "enjoyed *again.*"

Most interesting, however, are the phrases in Reagan's speech that *seem* to be positively forward looking, but that actually reflect highly ambivalent or middle-ground positions – a sort of two-way road signs of progression and retrogression combined. When he suggests that "America is much improved," for example, his expression (which almost has an advertising ring to it) straddles both "old" and "new."

And, if the sentence "Americans were ready to make a *new beginning*" is something more than mere tautology, it evokes at the same time the idea of repetition *(beginning once more)*. Reagan's allegiance to a "reconstruction" philosophy also assumes almost religious connotations, as for example in phrases like "spiritual **re**vival" and "crusade for **re**newal," where the prefixes nonetheless make them function very much like the clause "It's time to move *forward again*" – words which point, as it were, backward and forward at one and the same time. Similarly, with a metaphorical turn of phrase like "The *tide* of the future is a freedom *tide*," one cannot but be reminded of the fact that a "tide" may designate not only something that flows, but also something that both flows and ebbs. And the following passage towards the end of Reagan's address is pure paradox: "After all our struggles to *restore* America, to *revive* confidence in our country . . . we can*not*, must *not* and will *not* turn *back*": surely ideas of restoration and revival evoke, at the very same time, the sense of someone wanting to reinstate that which was before (an American pre-welfare state society, perhaps).

In short, a close discourse analysis of the extended interplay of these "old/new" semantic features in Reagan's rhetoric produces the impression of a President who cannot quite make up his mind whether he wants to live in the past or the present, and who can only conceive of his country's future in terms of its past. Of course Reagan's declamatory strategy of "the new" makes his conservatism seem dynamic and attractive. In my opinion, however, it is more than a rhetorical device; his constant vacillation between a past-oriented and a future-oriented frame of mind reflects an important schism in American culture in general – the ideological rupture between a past-oriented *laissez-faire* ideology and a strong belief in social progress and the possibility of change.

The main objective of this presentation of a cultural linguistics (which must include syntactics, morphology, pragmatics, semantics, and discourse analysis) has been to demonstrate that language and culture are inextricably connected. As a discipline within the study of English, culture studies must make the analysis of language uses part of its central cognitive concerns. It is the familiarity with *both* cultural ideas *and* the way they are expressed which in the study of English lays the foundation for understanding as well as proficiency. As Clifford Geertz puts it: "The whole point of a semiotic approach to culture is . . . to aid us in gaining access to the conceptual world in which our subjects live so that we can, in some extended sense of the term, converse with them."[26]

Notes

1 See Ferdinand de Saussure, *Course in General Linguistics* (New York: Philosophical Library, 1959); and Noam Chomsky, *Syntactic Structures* (The Hague: Mouton, 1957).
2 Fish, *Is There a Text in This Class?* (Cambridge, Mass.: Harvard Univ. Press, 1980), p. 284.
3 Fowler, "The Structure of Criticism and the Languages of Poetry: An Approach through Language," in Malcolm Bradbury and David Palmer, eds., *Contemporary Criticism* (London: Edward Arnold, 1970), p. 185.
4 See for example Halliday, *Explorations in the Functions of Language* (London: Edward Arnold, 1973).
5 For a brief survey of the main concerns in sociolinguistics, see Peter Trudgill, *Sociolinguistics: An Introduction* (Harmondsworth: Penguin, 1974).
6 Highly interesting for their discussion and analysis of the relationship between language, ideology, and power are Gunther Kress and Robert Hodge, *Language as Ideology* (London: Routledge & Kegan Paul, 1979), and Roger Fowler, Bob Hodge, Gunther Kress, and Tony Trew, *Language and Control* (London: Routledge & Kegan Paul, 1979).
7 See Austin, *How to Do Things with Words* (Cambridge, Mass.: Harvard Univ. Press, 1962); Searle, *Speech Acts: An Essay in the Philosophy of Language* (Cambridge: Cambridge Univ. Press, 1969); and Searle, "Indirect Speech Acts," and Paul H. Grice, "Logic and Conversation," both in Peter Cole and Jerry L. Morgan, eds., *Syntax and Semantics*, vol. III: *Speech Acts* (New York: Academic Press, 1975), pp. 59-82 and 41-58, respectively. For a general linguistic introduction, see Geoffrey N. Leech, *Principles of Pragmatics* (London: Longman, 1983).
8 Widdowson, *Explorations in Applied Linguistics* (Oxford: Oxford Univ. Press, 1979), p. 90; see his discussion of discourse on pp. 87-100 and 112-149.
9 Labov, *Sociolinguistic Patterns* (Philadelphia: Univ. of Pennsylvania Press, 1972), pp. 120-121.
10 Fowler, p. 186 (see note 3).
11 Halliday, *Language as Social Semiotic: The Social Interpretation of Language and Meaning* (London: Edward Arnold, 1978), pp. 52, 57.
12 The example, but not the interpretation, is from Kress and Hodge, *Language as Ideology*, p. 112 (see note 6).
13 Reagan, "State of the Union Address," 1984, in *Historic Documents of 1984* (Washington, D.C.: Congressional Quarterly, 1985), p. 86.
14 Reagan's 1984 Address, p. 91.
15 Reagan's 1984 Address, pp. 85, 87.
16 Kress and Hodge, p. 8 (see note 6).
17 Kress and Hodge, p. 27 (see note 6).
18 Reagan's 1984 Address, pp. 87, 90.
19 Kress and Hodge, p. 27. See also the excellent discussion of the use of nominal and passive constructions in Fowler, Hodge, Kress, and Trew, *Language and Control*, particularly Fowler and Kress's chapters "Rules and Regulations," pp. 26-45, and "Critical Linguistics," pp. 185-213 (see note 6).
20 Reagan's 1984 Address, p. 85.
21 See Kress and Hodge, *Language as Ideology*, p. 27, and Fowler, Hodge, Kress, and Trew, *Language and Control*, p. 31 (see note 6).
21 Reagan's 1984 Address, p. 85.
22 Sandemose, *Rejsen til Kørkelvik* (Copenhagen: Hans Reitzel, 1954), pp. 103-104 (my translation).
23 Reagan's 1984 Address, p. 85.
24 Reagan's 1984 Address, pp. 85, 86, 87, 89, 90, 91, 95.
25 Geertz, *The Interpretation of Cultures* (New York: Basic Books, 1973), p. 24.

5

The «Literariness« of Ordinary Language: Culture Studies as a Literary-oriented Discipline

The study of linguistic discourse is not the subject of linguistics only; it is also the main concern of literary studies. This chapter will therefore discuss what a *literary* approach to the study of language may contribute to the cultural analysis of "non-literary" texts. In this connection, it should be pointed out that the failure to integrate the disciplines of linguistics, culture studies, and literary studies within the subject of English has not only been a result of the exclusively formalist approach in linguistics or the exclusively fact-oriented "background" approach in the study of civilization. The lack of integration has also been a product of the theories of literary autonomy – not least as propagated by the school of the New Criticism, which dominated the study of literature particularly in the l950s and 60s.

It was above all the concept of the organic unity of the literary work that made many New Critics regard literature as autonomous. As the various formal features of a literary work were seen mutually to give meaning to each other so as to form a self-contained whole, the central task of literary explication was the intrinsic analysis of this carefully composed totality. The study of history and society was to a large extent considered superfluous to understanding the work, and biographical information was often regarded as irrelevant.

A student of cultural texts would not necessarily reject the idea that a text may represent a unified whole. He would argue, however, that this whole is by no means self-contained. Instead, it must itself be regarded as a social and cultural product. Of course, different formal features in a text may mutually define and modify each other, but to the historical-oriented student the very character of their interplay is culturally conditioned. The formal organization of different means of expression may thus be seen as the work's expression of, and reaction to, the culture in which it is written. Familiarity with historical context thus becomes an interpretive prerequisite.

"Literary" vs. "Ordinary" Language

Many New Critics also argued, however, that literary language was in itself different from non-literary or "ordinary" uses of language. Ordinary conversation or prose was, for example, regarded as predominantly literal and referential, whereas literary language was seen as metaphorical and imaginative. It is highly doubtful, however, whether it is possible or even useful to operate with such principal distinctions. Figurative and "poetic" means of expression are of course found outside literature, too, which is one of the reasons why we recognize and take pleasure in them in literature as well.

It is certainly true, as a general observation, that the language of imaginative literature is often more suggestive than "ordinary" uses of language, but this is a matter of degree, not of kind. Of course, some literary texts, like those of lyrical poetry, tend to make use of a highly evocative and metaphorical style, but this is less true of novels, particularly realist ones. And, although a scholarly essay may be predominantly discursive, political speeches, personal letters, or advertising texts may make use of highly emotional and figurative means of expression. On the level of language use only, it is often hard to distinguish between literary and non-literary representation. Take the following sentence: "In my younger and more vulnerable years my father gave me some advice that I've been turning over in my mind ever since." Does this language in any particular way signal that we here deal with imaginative literature? Or take the following statement: "This is just to say I have eaten the plums that were in the icebox, and which you were probably saving for breakfast. Forgive me. They were delicious, so sweet and so cold." Is this language particularly "literary"? It so happens that both examples are taken from canonical literary texts; the former case represents the first sentence of F. Scott Fitzgerald's *The Great Gatsby*, and the latter is a poem by William Carlos Williams – shorn of its division into verse lines and with punctuation marks added.[1] In these particular cases, there are obviously no intrinsic language characteristics that mark the two sentences off as "literary" rather than "non-literary."

Sometimes fictionality is used as a criterion for distinguishing between literary and non-literary works, but as I will argue in the next chapter, all texts must be viewed as being figurative as well as referential – they all serve to construct as well as reflect our experience. Again, the distinction is a tenuous one. The same is true of the argument that literary texts represent a distinct category of writing because of their highly wrought structure. Other kinds of writing are also deliberately structured – including this chapter or, say, a treatise in philosophy or a feature in a magazine.

Even if we limit the subject to particular literary genres, it is difficult to come up with absolute distinctions. One may be tempted to argue that lyrical poetry, at least, is graphically distinctive in terms of its broken verse lines, like in Williams's "This Is Just to Say":

I have eaten
the plums
that were in
the icebox

but what does one then do about the text of an advertisement written like this:

Regina Porter
Blouses.
They'll Take
You Anywhere![2]

In terms of language use only, the latter stanza is certainly not less evocative than the first one by Williams. The crux of the matter is that Williams's poem could, if we so desired, be analyzed as part of an advertisement for plums, and the blouse advertisement could, if we so desired, be read as a poem. Nothing we may do with these texts will unearth some linguistic principle according to which we may define one as "literary" and the other as "non-literary." In these examples, it is the knowledge of the contexts in which they appear, or the frame of mind of the reader, that will determine the classification.

This is not to say that it is impossible to evolve sets of intrinsic and extrinsic criteria for classifying works of imaginative literature *vis-à-vis* other texts, but these must be multiple and non-categorical. More important for the subsequent discussion, however, is the fact that there are no features of language which, in principle, can distinguish between them. A wide variety of language uses is found outside imaginative literature as well. In everyday life people certainly appreciate a clever turn of phrase, and use language in order to catch attention and to hold it. We all know how small children often play and experiment with language, and how adults converse at a pleasant party when jokes, puns, and stories start to flourish. It is hardly an exaggeration to suggest that entertaining people, regardless of their age, are not first and foremost appreciated for their literalness, but for their, well, "literariness."

The technique of foregrounding language through striking usages is consequently part of everyday speech and writing – the formalist theories of imaginative literature notwithstanding. As Mary Louise Pratt put it some ten years ago, "throughout the brilliant body of Formalist scholarship on prose fiction, nary a scholar seriously poses the question of whether or to what extent devices like palpableness of form, estrangement, foregrounding, and laying bare of devices exist outside literature." Her own work, *Toward a Speech Act Theory of Literary Discourse,* demonstrates convincingly that language in ordinary social interaction makes use of many of the same formal devices as do literary genres, and that they indeed can be analyzed, structurally and aesthetically, in much the same way. As Pratt puts it when discussing "natural narratives," this "casts grave doubt on the Formalist and structuralist claims that the language of literature is formally and functionally distinctive."[3] There is consequently no reason to view literary works only as élitist phenomena divorced from everyday cultural activities; they may be regarded as highly literate and articulate expressions of modes of perception that are deeply ingrained in cultural life in general. This point of view may indirectly serve to legitimize the role played by literary studies within the study of English as a foreign language; at the same time, it implies that the analysis of literary means of expression is necessary for the field of culture studies as well.

Cultural Simile, Metaphor, Symbol

As I have discussed the subject of cultural semantics in Chapter 4 on "Culture and Language," what remains to be examined here is not so much the use of connotative language in general as the function of particular "poetic" figures of speech with which literary studies have dealt extensively, but which has received relatively little attention in conventional linguistic or historical studies. The most important of such figurative means of expression are those of *simile, metaphor,* and *symbol*. Whole books within philosophy and literary studies have been written on the subject of these,[4] but for the purposes of the practical interpretation of non-literary texts, we may simply define *simile* as an explicit comparison between two dissimilar things ("My love is *like* a red rose"), *metaphor* as a suggested identification or imaginative merging of two different things ("My love *is* a red rose"), and *symbol* as a sign that stands for something else (the *rose* as an icon of erotic love, for example). These figures of speech represent techniques of elucidation by which we refer to something in terms of something else from another domain of experience, often by giving abstract ideas a concrete form, or by presenting something unfamiliar by way of something familiar, or, inversely, by imbuing conventional signs with new meaning. Sometimes the effect of such tropological transformations is that of simplification, sometimes that of an expansion, of meaning. As Susanne K. Langer puts it, for example, the use of metaphor is the power "whereby new words are born and merely analogical meanings become stereotyped into literal definitions. . . . It is the force that makes it [language] essentially *relational,* intellectual, forever showing up new, abstractable *forms* in reality, forever laying down a deposit of old, abstracted concepts in an increasing treasure of general words."[5]

5 – Culture, Language,...

It may be useful, however, to differentiate between the use of simile and metaphor on the one hand and that of symbol on the other. Similes and metaphors are purely linguistic constructions, whereas a cultural symbol is often a non-linguistic sign as well as a figure of speech. Similes/metaphors and symbols can also be distinguished from one another in terms of their function and import. A simile or a metaphor has the function of elucidating something in the immediate context in which it is used. In order for a sign to be designated as a symbol, however, I would suggest that it must be of importance to a much larger frame of reference and be used in various connections, by which it acquires a rich suggestiveness. Thus, a cultural symbol or the symbol in a novel is a sign that is important for the culture at large or the novel as a whole – an image that, by way of its recurrence in different contexts, becomes a structural nucleus and a thematic repository for a range of different ideas and associations. If we take the sign *cross* as an illustration, we see how it may serve as the expression of the whole continuum from literal to highly figurative usages: it may represent a denotation (two lines crossing each other); an index (indicating a grave); a connotation (for example "death" or "sorrow"); a metaphor (in which the tenor is latent, for example "the cross of poverty"), and a symbol (the way it is central to Christianity, for example).

All cultural texts, albeit in varying degrees, make use of figurative means of expression, such as similes, metaphors, and symbols. When for example the Secretary of the Treasury under President Ford, William E. Simon, declared that "the public should not be fleeced of taxes to keep any business alive that, like the dinosaur, has outlived its usefulness,"[6] the simile of social Darwinism carries the implications of something natural and inevitable, hence something acceptable and to some extent (with the idea of natural selection) even positive. (This is emphasized also by the negative implication of the metaphorical phrase "fleeced of taxes," which refers us to the domain of animal imagery while evoking connotations of robbery and fraud). Similarly, when for example President Ford argued in April 1975 for more money to the Thieu regime, he suggested that the tragedy of the development of the war in Vietnam was the result of the fact that the United States had not made a special effort "'at the last minute of the last quarter.'"[7] This football metaphor, as Thomas H. Middleton observed, "puts war in the same class with sport," implying that "the Vietnam War had a time limit and that if we could throw in that final burst of weaponry, 'our guys' might snatch victory from the jaws of defeat before the old clock on the scoreboard counted down to 'no seconds left' . . .'"[8] Sports imagery of this type is not only a means of presenting complex sociohistorical problems in terms of the simplicity of a rule-governed game, it also gives expression to the American cultural preoccupation with competitiveness and winning.

This production of multiple associations is even more extensive in the case of cultural symbols. The image of the machine in 19th century American life is a case in point, evoking the idea of a mechanized society and of society itself as a machine. On the one hand, the figure of the machine served to connote order and systematic progress (with the implications of something smoothly functioning, well-oiled, and manageable); on the other hand, it also became expressive of people's sense of powerlessness and alienation in an increasingly technological society (with the implications of something threatening, impersonal, and liable to break down.) As Leo Marx and others have shown, even in the era of triumphant industrialism there was also a masked pattern of fear of mechanization, of machines taking control like Frankenstein monsters, destroying the natural garden of society.[9] In this manner, a cultural symbol often becomes the concrete nucleus for complex and conflicting culture patterns. A particular version of a cultural symbol may in some cases serve as an impetus for sociopolitical change, but a symbol may equally well embody quite ambivalent significations and thus serve to maintain the status quo. As James W. Fernandez puts it, "who can deny that there are many subtle things to be said about the work of metaphor and symbol? Strategies may often end in poetry, perhaps the ultimate strategy, where instead of being moved anywhere we are accommodated in many subtle ways to our condition in all its contrarieties and complexities."[10]

The last observation may present a rather disputable view of the function of poetry, but with such a thesis of metaphor and symbol we have in a sense moved along a discursive continuum that leads from ethics to aesthetics. It may be suggested that dominant symbols, in and outside textual sources, also serve an aesthetic function. If we define aesthetic effect as the way by which the signs of our experience (in life or art) acquire coherence, fuse thought and emotion, and conjoin several dominant, even disparate, ideas, then the use of collective cultural images has an aesthetic dimension. According to Gertrude Jaeger and Philip Selznick, genuine cultural symbols are polysemous and "provide that shading of connotative meanings without which the symbol would degenerate, that is, trigger a reaction rather than evoke a response."[11]

If, as the above discussion suggests, figurative means of expression are also of fundamental importance for cultural discourse, then the insights produced by language philosophers and literary critics must be acquired in order to analyze their function. As Clifford Geertz puts it in an essay on "Ideology as a Cultural System,"

With no notion of how metaphor, analogy, irony, ambiguity, pun, paradox, hyperbole, rhythm, and all the other elements of what we lamely call "style" operate – even, in a majority of cases, with no recognition that these devices are of any importance in casting personal attitudes into public form, sociologists lack the symbolic resources out of which to construct a more incisive formulation.[12]

An analytical understanding of a wide range of literary means of expression is consequently necessary for the study of culture, though space prohibits that they all be discussed here.

Cultural Narrative

A central "literary" phenomenon, which Geertz does not mention above and which nevertheless deserves some separate comment, is the cultural use of *narrative*. The telling of stories also plays an essential part in everyday cultural life. Narratives pervade people's daily lives as well as the affairs presented on television, in newspapers and in magazines: stories about the "real truth" of Elvis's last years at Graceland; about the power struggle in the Republican or Democratic party before the next election; about a woman's indefatigable fight against her child's incurable disease; about a wife's gullibility all those times her husband reportedly worked late at the office; and so on and so forth. More importantly, people themselves constantly tell others – spouses and friends and anybody who will listen – about what they have heard and thought, about what has happened to themselves or others, and others tell similar stories to them.

Thus we are not only surrounded by stories, we live to a great extent *through* stories, and *in* stories – stories that we spin out of the chronicles of the world and the biography of our own lives. In his introduction to *Mind and Nature: A Necessary Unity,* Gregory Bateson tells the story of a man who asked his computer: "Do you compute that you will ever think like a human being?" to which the computer finally printed out its answer: "THAT REMINDS ME OF A STORY."[13] In Greek and Latin the word for *history* and *story* was the same, meaning a narrative, a tale (originally designating both real and imaginary ones) – and the two words are still identical in, for example, modern French *(histoire),* German *(Geschichte),* and Scandinavian *(historie).* As we all to a considerable extent view the world in terms of stories, the borderlines between history, language, and "literary" techniques become fluid indeed.

In his book *Language in the Inner City: Studies in the Black English Vernacular,* William Labov shows for instance that fully developed oral narratives among black youth evinced the following structure: 1) abstract (initial summary of the story); 2) orientation (setting the story in terms of situation, time, place, and actors); 3) complicating action; 4) evaluation (indicating the point of the narrative); 5) result or resolution; and 6) coda (signalling that the narrative is finished). Not all these elements were part of every narrative, and the evaluation was sometimes produced by various means of expression throughout the narrative, but Labov found that a great many of these oral narratives followed a close-knit, skilfully structured pattern: "Many of the narratives cited here rise to a very high level of competence; when they are quoted in the exact words of the speaker, they will command the total attention of an audience in a remarkable way, creating a deep and attentive silence that is never found in academic or political discussion. The reaction of listeners to these narratives seems to demonstrate that the most highly evaluated form of language is that which translates our personal experience into dramatic form."[14] The structure of these narratives is not unlike that which literary students learn to recognize in their study of imaginative fiction or drama, with elements like exposition, development and complication of the plot, peripeteia/climax, and resolution/denouement.

The structural and thematic implications of popular narratives in a culture have received far too little attention in culture studies. What people choose to focus on in their own lives and in the lives of other people is an important testimony to their mode of thinking. Every culture embodies collective myths, prominent story formulas which, in various versions, are told over and over again. Even a "true-story" tear-jerker from *Reader's Digest* may sometimes bring us closer to the world view of many Americans than would an analytical feature from *Time* or *Newsweek*. The same is true of popular fiction: a hard-boiled detective story may for example – precisely in terms of its type of characters, plot, and style – be an important source for the analysis of dominant assumptions in American society. Similarly with the myths about the American pioneer, the mountain man, the cowboy, or the rags-to-riches entrepreneur: popular narratives about these figures and their more contemporary counterparts are concrete dramatizations of core American values, and should be analyzed both for their structure, their idiom, and their themes (such as those of individualism, self-reliance, and winning).

Three Cultural Texts Analyzed in Literary Terms

In order to concretize these theoretical observations, the rest of this chapter will be devoted to the analysis of three texts – one primarily for its narrative form and two for their use of metaphorical means of expression. The first story is taken from Richard Nixon's acceptance speech when nominated as the Republican Presidential candidate in Miami in 1968. After having discoursed extensively on the state of affairs in America, and after mentioning briefly that millions of American children live in poverty, Nixon launched into a narrative:

> But this is only part of what I see in America. I see another child tonight. He hears the train go by at night, and dreams of faraway places where he'd like to go. It seems like an impossible dream. But he is helped on his journey through life. A father who had to go to work before he finished the sixth grade sacrificed everything he had so that his sons could go to college. A gentle Quaker mother with a passionate concern for peace quietly wept when he went to war, but she understood why he had to go. A great teacher, a remarkable football coach, an inspirational minister encouraged him on his way. A courageous wife and loyal children stood by him in victory and also in defeat. And in his chosen profession of politics, first there were scores, then hundreds, then thousands, and finally millions who worked for his success. And tonight he stands before you nominated for President of the United States of America.
>
> You can see why I believe so deeply in the American dream. For most of us the American revolution has been won, the American dream has come true. And what I ask you to do tonight is to help me make that dream come true for millions to whom it's an impossible dream today.[15]

This is a miniature version of the rags-to-riches formula story, with a beginning in very modest or poor circumstances, a middle of struggle and conflict (war, college, victory, and defeat), and an ending with final achievement.

At an even more general level, Nixon's story evinces many of the structural characteristics of the conventional fairy tale, with a hero who seeks an object (in this case success) and who is helped and hindered on his way. The helpers (whose numbers increase from two to millions) in Nixon's narrative are, as in the fairy tale, not important for their individual characteristics but for their function in the plot. Thus, the story includes "a" father whose (masculine) ethos of self-denial and self-reliance leads him to postpone gratification to ensure his son's future success, and "a" mother whose (feminine) virtues of gentleness and "concern for peace" presumably sustain him when he has to venture into a world of war. In addition, there are "a" "courageous wife and loyal children" who stand by him. The use of the indefinite or zero article in all these cases serves to indicate that the role of these helpers is generically cultural rather than personal; they represent the family archetypes of Nixon's middle-class "silent majority" who do not look to the government for help. Equally generic are the other helpers specified in Nixon's narrative; they are representatives of the three most cherished repositories of values in American culture: "A great teacher" (education), "a remarkable football coach" (sport as a means of learning fair play and competitiveness), and "an inspirational minister" (religion). These three exemplary cultural models are found in countless American success formulas, for example in many Horatio Alger stories.

As analyzed in a classical study by Vladimir Propp, the plot structure of the conventional fairy tale also embodies some character roles that are absent in Nixon's narrative – for reasons that are relatively obvious. Traditional tales usually involve one or more villains who try to stop the hero from reaching his goal (but Nixon's present situation demands that he unite, not split, his party by telling about them), and they also often include a donor or provider for the hero (but it would be unwise of Nixon to bring the subject of donorship into a tale that celebrates the myth of equal opportunity).[16]

At the end, the story of Nixon's journey from "impossible" childhood dreams to his being nominated a Presidential candidate is explicitly identified by Nixon himself as a *particular* cultural narrative, that of the American Dream, according to which anyone with pluck and drive can one day become "President of the United States of America." The formal technique of the third person point of view, as well as the repeated use of generic references, make Nixon's tale almost assume the character of a fable; it is this legend-like air that makes the moral at the end almost appropriate and acceptable (its misrepresentation notwithstanding): "For most of us the American revolution has been won, the American dream has come true."

The main point of this analysis, however, is to emphasize that the ideals of equal opportunity and success are widespread and pervasive in American culture not merely because they exist as ideas, but because they exist as *myth* – that is, as cultural narratives, in imaginative-dramatic form. As W. Lloyd Warner put it in *Social Class in America* (1949):

> From grade school on, we have learned to cite chapter and verse proving from the lives of many of the great men of American history that we can start at the bottom and climb to the highest peaks of achievement when we have a few brains and a will to do. Our mass magazines and newspapers print and reprint the legendary story of rags to riches and tell over and over again the Ellis-Island-to-Park-Avenue saga in the actual lives of contemporary successful immigrant men and women. From mere repetition, it might be thought that the public would tire of the theme; the names are all

that vary and the stories, like those of children, remain the same. But we never do tire of this theme, for it says what we need to know and what we want to hear.[17]

Again one may add, however, that it is not simply the popularity of this cultural theme that makes people interested in it; it is also its "literary" form, its transformation of social aspiration into chronicle and tale where the listeners or readers take pleasure both in the recognition of a familiar story formula and in its particular realization – its specific versions of struggles and resolutions, heroes and villains, helpers and donors. In addition, as in Nixon's story, there is the rhetorical evocation of a particular cultural melodrama: a hero hearing "the train go by" and dreaming of "faraway places"; an uneducated, hard-working father sacrificing "everything he had"; a Quaker mother "quietly" weeping when her son "went to war"; and so on and so forth. This – however formulaic, and precisely because it is formulaic – is the stuff that culture is made of. This is also a reason why all types of cultural texts should be the object of critical analysis and interpretation within the humanities.

The theme of the second text is also one of success. It is excerpted from the cover story in *Esquire* from November 1983 and deals with Sanford Weill, President of the American Express Company, and his "appetite" for acquiring companies and arranging corporate mergers. The following passages are particularly interesting for their metaphorical imagery, through which particular meanings are attributed to business dealings:

**When Shearson ate Loeb Rhoades
and American Express ate
Shearson, Sanford Weill ate well.
Now he's insatiable.**
- - - - -

Weill is constantly probing for information: poking around, asking plenty of questions about the weaknesses and strengths of prospective acquistitions. He is a boxer, not a street fighter, searching for the safest opening. And he was never lighter on his feet, nor more determined, than when he was stalking American Express.
- - - - -

Weill's impulses are more than a little Machiavellian. He had actually first approached Amexco informally in 1975, sending out a feeler through an executive vice-president but never got a response. It was not until he met Robinson in September of 1980 that he got a second shot. Robinson had been at Amexco when Weill had made his last pass but this was the first he heard of Weill's interest in the company. Though Weill did not talk openly with Robinson about a merger, he was prepared to act quickly, and when Prudential became, effectively, the first superbroker by acquiring Bache the following March, he moved reflexively to start negotiations with American Express.

- - - - -

"It was known at the firm," says John Sullivan, who was a Shearson executive after Weill acquired his firm, Faulkner, Dawkins & Sullivan, "that he takes no prisoners. Even some top people who made mistakes found themselves out of a job."[18]

In these passages, the world of business is metaphorically envisioned in terms of the world of predatory animals, hunting, sport, and war. First of all, Weill's success in business acquisitions is likened to appetite: "When Shearson ate Loeb Rhoades and American Express ate Shearson, Sanford Weill ate well. Now he's insatiable." Such a metaphorical evocation of physiological urges transfers the concept of ambition from being a social phenomenon to becoming a fundamental drive which one can do little about, except to satisfy it. In addition, this imagery also brings to mind the philosophy of "eat or be eaten," evoking a Darwinist world of predatory animals where only the fittest survive. A related physiological implication also surfaces at the end, when Weill is described as moving "reflexively" (not "reflectively") "to start negotiations," suggesting that his actions are almost instinctive.

The idea of moving by reflex may also be linked with the dominant strain of sport-and-warfare metaphors in these passages. Weill is described as "a boxer," "searching for the safest openings," and being light "on his feet." He is also said to get "a second shot" at the acquisition, which evokes ball sports; it may also, however, be linked to the recurring images of hunting and warfare, as when Weill is portrayed as "stalking" American Express and as taking "no prisoners" once he has acquired a firm. Through the use of these metaphorical means of expression, the vision of business becomes a highly ambiguous one. On the one hand, the sports imagery makes business competition seem like a game (Weill as a "boxer, not a street fighter") – a rule-governed play, an image that serves to obscure its actual social, economic, and human consequences. On the other hand, the predatory images and the warfare metaphors make business into a matter of uncivilized, cutthroat competition; in a paradoxical fashion, however, they also function to legitimize the ruthlessness of business at the same time. The hunting metaphor occupies a kind of intermediary position; it may evoke gamesmanship, but it may also connote slaughter. *Laissez-faire* economics as envisioned here thus assumes the form of the law of the jungle – at one and the same time something rule-governed and regulated and something unbridled and anarchic. In addition, these kinds of metaphors imply that business enterprise is a matter of individualist competition and winning, rather than a matter of a cooperative endeavor.

This type of sport, hunting and warfare imagery is fairly common in American culture for describing the life of business or politics; the Watergate tapes of Nixon's White House conversations, for example, abounded with such metaphors. As my analysis here has attempted to illustrate, the objective of the study of such metaphorical figures of speech is to elucidate the cultural *way of thinking* that they serve to embody. Thus, as James W. Fernandez points out, the study of metaphor is also of central importance in cultural analysis:

> While I first felt sheepish about taking up the problem of metaphor in the social sciences, I now feel more bullish. At least we should have been tossed on the horns of the following dilemma which I believe fundamental to the understanding of culture. However men may analyze their experiences within any domain, they inevitably know and understand them best by referring them to other domains for elucidation.[19]

One may add, however, that this process of "elucidation" is a double-edged sword; metaphors may also be used to simplify and even obscure actual sociocultural processes. This is particularly true of the language of the third text for discussion – the two-line caption of an advertisement for Max Factor *Epris* cologne, which may serve as the concluding illustration of the importance of a "literary" approach to the study of culture. The illustration features a half-length close-up of the well-known American model Jaclyn Smith in a semi-transparent dress, looking straight at the reader in a graceful, pretty and mildly sensuous fashion, accompanied by the following words[20]:

Part of the art of being a woman is knowing when not to be too much of a lady.

The basic thematic opposition in this slick aphorism seems to be that of "woman" vs. "lady," which is also foregrounded by the graphic-poetic line division of the text. When contrasted to "woman," the concept of "lady" may connote someone with good breeding and education, someone cultivated and refined – in short, the female as a sociocultural product, well-bred and house-trained. The phrase may even evoke associations like "The Lady of the Manor," "the lady of the house," or "Our Lady": the first connoting aristocracy, the second housewifery, and the third religion and virginity. In all these cases, "lady" refers to the female's public and conventional role, perhaps to someone who is morally beyond reproach.

By contrast, the concept of "woman" evokes personal rather than social role connotations, particularly with regard to sexuality (the fragrance of the cologne is described as "most provocative"): woman as lover rather than wife, mistress rather than Mrs. Thus, it may be suggested that the fundamental dichotomies involved here are those of

$$\frac{\text{woman}}{\text{lady}} \approx \frac{\text{individual}}{\text{society}} \approx \frac{\text{sex}}{\text{class}} \approx \frac{\text{nature}}{\text{culture}}$$

Thus, in structuralist terms, the basic semantic isotopies behind these classes of semes[21] are those of nature vs. culture, something natural vs. something artificial. Consequently the perfume and the woman in the illustration also become identified with that which is not conventional, that which is sensual. (There is no rampant sexuality suggested here, however; sensuality is only "part of" being a woman, a matter of avoiding being "too much" of a lady.)

The identification of the product with some "natural" sensuality is probably the "message" that any reader more or less consciously gets from this advertisement, but it is only its most direct implication. The text of the advertisement is more devious than that. If "being a woman" had only been a matter of being natural and artless, then there would, strictly speaking, be no reason for her to use a perfume at all. But the advertisement actually presents its theme in terms of a *metaphor*, in terms of *the art of being a woman,* which suggests that *woman* is not something she is by definition; it is the product of an art – something which, first of all, is skilfully made, and something which, secondly, connotes beauty. The phrase "the art of being" is thus quite paradoxical; what is actually evoked here is not so much a state of being, as a technique of transformation. To be a woman involves a formative skill, as womanhood is not something naturally given but, instead, something that one consciously constructs by making oneself attractive.

Through the use of this metaphor, the text thus contradicts and deconstructs itself and becomes pure paradox: "Part of the artfulness of being a woman is knowing when not to be too artful," or, "Part of being a cultural construct is knowing when not to be too much of a cultural construct." At the same time, however, the sentence makes perfect sense; it is quite representative of the culture of advertising language in which the sign of *the natural* has lost its connection with an actual referent and has turned into pure signifier: Like other signs, such as *fresh* and *pure,* the word *natural* merely connotes a synthetic-cultural, life-*like* construct. More specifically, this advertising text is a perfectly appropriate expression of the ideology that is built into the language and pictures of countless cosmetics advertisements, making the concept of woman into something that is self-consciously *made up* by way of precisely *make-up* and other beauty aids. Thus, in American society as well as in other Western cultures, a woman is often not seen to be a woman by force of her sex, the way "a man is a man"; she is required to use artful means in order to mould herself into a gender-specific image with which others want her to identify. In sum, the metaphor discussed here, buried, as it were, in the deep structure of the text, is the embodiment of an ideology that seeks – in this case subtly, in the guise of the theme of an unladylike non-conventionality – to reduce one half of the population to artful ornaments and/or sexual objects.

Thus, the seemingly simple, "non-literary" sentence "Part of the art of being a woman/is knowing when not to be too much of a lady" engenders a web of multiple meanings which can best be sorted out by a systematic "literary-oriented" approach – by an awareness of how images and metaphors function as figurative means of expression in speech and writing. Without it, the cultural analysis of texts may all too often scratch only the surface of their multiple significations. The use of words is inevitably a manyfaceted and equivocal matter which, for better or for worse, is by far our most important means of cultural expression and interpretation. As Clifford Geertz puts it, culture studies is basically about the interpretation of "meaningful forms," and these, be they African passage rites, revolutionary ideologies, landscape paintings, or "the ways in which moral judgments are phrased,"

> have as good a claim to public existence as horses, stones, and trees, and are therefore as susceptible to objective investigation and systematic analysis as these apparently harder realities. . . . It may be supremely difficult to deal with such structures of meaning but they are neither a miracle nor a mirage. Indeed, constructing concepts and methods to deal with them and to produce generalizations about them is the primary intellectual task now facing those humanists and social scientists not content merely to exercise habitual skills.[22]

Notes

1 Fitzgerald, *The Great Gatsby* (New York: Scribner's, 1925), p. 1; and Williams, "This Is Just to Say," *The Collected Earlier Poems of William Carlos Williams* (New York: New Directions, 1966), p. 354.
2 Advertisement for "Regina Porter Blouses," *Cosmopolitan*, 196, no. 5 (November 1983), 13.

3. Mary Louise Pratt, *Toward a Speech Act Theory of Literary Discourse* (Bloomington: Indiana Univ. Press, 1977), pp. 5, 67.
4. A particularly incisive work on metaphor is Paul Ricoeur's *The Rule of Metaphor: Multi-disciplinary Studies of the Creation of Meaning in Language* (London: Routledge & Kegan Paul, 1977).
5. Langer, *Philosophy in a New Key* (Cambridge, Mass.: Harvard Univ. Press, 1957; first published 1942), p. 141.
6. Quoted in John Minahan, "Is 'Free Market' a Dirty Word? An Interview with the Secretary of the Treasury," *Saturday Review*, July 12, 1975, p. 19.
7. Quoted in Thomas H. Middleton, "The Great Muddling Metaphor," *Saturday Review*, June 14, 1975, p. 59.
8. Middleton, p. 59.
9. See Bernard Bowron, Leo Marx, and Arnold Rose, "Literature and Covert Culture," in Joseph J. Kwiat and Mary C. Turpie, eds., *Studies in American Culture: Dominant Ideas and Images* (Minneapolis: Univ. of Minnesota Press, 1960), pp. 84-95; and Marx, *The Machine in the Garden* (New York: Oxford Univ. Press, 1964).
10. Fernandez, "Persuasions and Performances: Of the Beast in Every Body... And the Metaphors of Everyman," in Clifford Geertz, ed., *Myth, Symbol, and Culture* (New York: Norton, 1971), p. 53.
11. Jaeger and Selznick, "A Normative Theory of Culture," in Robert Merideth, ed., *American Studies: Essays on Theory and Method* (Columbus, Ohio: Charles E. Merrill, 1968), p. 115.
12. Geertz, "Ideology as a Cultural System," *The Interpretation of Cultures* (New York: Basic Books, 1973), p. 209.
13. Bateson, *Mind and Nature* (New York: Bantam Books, 1979), p. 14.
14. Labov, *Language in the Inner City: Studies in the Black English Vernacular* (Oxford: Blackwell, 1972), pp. 362-370, 396.
15. Richard Nixon, "The Long Dark Night for America Is About to End" [his acceptance speech on being nominated Republican candidate for President], *U.S. News and World Report*, August 19, 1968, p. 77.
16. See Vladimir Propp, *Morphology of the Folktale* (Austin: Univ. of Texas Press, 1968), particularly pp. 78-83.
17. Warner, *Social Class in America* (Chicago: Science Research Associates, 1949), p. 4.
18. Barry Rehfeld, "Deal Maker," *Esquire*, 100, no. 5 (November 1983), 86, 90, 94.
19. Fernandez, "Persuasions and Performances," p. 58 (see note 10).
20. Max Factor advertisement from *Cosmopolitan*, 195, no. 5 (November 1983), 41.
21. For a discussion of the terms "isotopy" and "classeme," see A.-J. Greimas, *Structural Semantics: An Attempt at a Method* (Lincoln: Univ. of Nebraska Press, 1983), particularly pp. 46-60 and 78-115.
22. Geertz, ed., *Myth, Symbol, and Culture*, pp. x, xi (see note 10).

6
Culture, History and Interpretation: Culture Studies as a Historical Discipline

As the discipline of culture studies involves the linguistic and literary analysis of world views embodied in texts, it may be related to fields such as the history of ideas and intellectual or cultural history. The concern in culture studies with belief systems as *representations of behavior,* however, makes history proper, and particularly social history, equally part of the undertaking; the analysis of dominant patterns of beliefs and values must be closely connected with the study of people's everyday lives and their actual socio-economic situation at a given time.

Explanation vs. Interpretation

With a stronger emphasis on documentation and objectivity than most other humanities disciplines, history has sometimes strived to emulate the methodical empiricism of the natural sciences. Traditionally, the "hard sciences" on the one side have often been distinguished from the "softer" humanities on the other, where the former deal "objectively" with the "explanation" of "facts" and the latter "subjectively" with the "interpretation" of "ideas." This distinction, however, is untenable and needs to be discussed before the importance of history for culture studies can be adequately examined.

Although some fields obviously make use of more empirically verifiable data than others, it must be made clear that the idea of a non-interpretive, exclusively factual "objectivity" is a myth. As Gunnar Myrdal points out in *An American Dilemma,* research in any field has to proceed from some hypothetical framework: "The chaos of possible data for research does not organize itself into systematic knowledge by mere observation. Hypotheses are necessary. . . . Even apparently simple concepts presume elaborate theories. These theories – or systems of hypotheses – contain, of necessity, no matter how scrupulously the statements of them are presented, elements of *a priori* speculation."[1]

The following exchange from one of Gregory Bateson's "metalogues" in *Steps to an Ecology of Mind* is quite instructive in this connection:

Daughter: Daddy, do you mean that Sir Isaac Newton thought that all hypotheses were just *made up* like stories?
Father: Yes – precisely that.
Daughter: But didn't he discover gravity? With the apple?
Father: No, dear. He invented it.[2]

Even in the physical and natural sciences, then, explanations are interpretive *constructions* imposed on certain types of data. As Thomas S. Kuhn argues in *The Structure of Scientific Revolutions,* whereas normal scientific research may be a matter of a cumulative progression of knowledge, the revolutionary shifts in dominant explanatory paradigms in the history of science are "not only incompatible but often actually incommensurable with that which has gone before" and involve at the same time changes in the entire world view of a scientific community. According to Kuhn it is therefore misleading to suggest that successive scientific theories give us a progressively "better representation of what nature is really like." As Kuhn suggests, instead of imagining "that there is some one full, objective, true account of nature and that the proper measure of scientific achievement is the extent to which it brings us closer to that ultimate goal," maybe we should "learn to substitute evolution-from-what-we-do-know for evolution-toward-what-we-wish-to-know." In this sense the so-called "hard" sciences ultimately involve the question of interpretation: the notion, as Kuhn puts it, "of a match between the ontology of a theory and its 'real' counterpart in nature now seems to me illusive in principle."[3]

The social sciences, history, and the other humanities fields are, however, distinctive in the sense that they deal directly with the study of meaning – with the analysis of various ways in which people conceive of their lives and their surroundings. Of course, purely behaviorist schools of psychology and sociology tried, particularly in the interwar years, to limit their study of man to observable facts, but as John Dewey suggested in *Freedom and Culture,* "Any doctrine that eliminates or even obscures the function of choice of values and enlistment of desires and emotions in behalf of those chosen weakens personal responsibility for judgment and for action."[4] Most theories of behavior in our own time have been anti-positivist as well as anti-behaviorist, suggesting that one cannot analyze conduct apart from the assumptions and motivations that guide and produce it. As A.L. Kroeber and Clyde Kluckhohn put it, an account of a culture without reference to its values would become "an unstructured, meaningless assemblance of items having relation to one another only through coexistence in locality and moment – an assemblage that might as profitably be arranged alphabetically as in any other order; a mere laundry list."[5]

This emphasis on beliefs and values in the social sciences in general and anthropology in particular has served to bring them much closer to the humanities, which have always dealt with cognitive and normative questions. Defined as patterns of assumptions and values that *guide* behavior, culture also implies, as Gertrude Jaeger and Philip Selznick put it, "a set of implicit and explicit standards which, in any society, can only be approximately embodied in action."[6] This idea of cultural norms imperfectly practiced parallels the concern in the humanities with the interplay between the ideal and the actual.

The social sciences and the humanities have traditionally been polarized in terms of their subject matter – the former dealing with "ordinary" culture and the latter with "élite" culture. Even in this respect, however, there has been a *rapprochement* over the last few decades. Humanities scholars, such as literary critics, art historians, and philosophers, have become more interested in studying phenomena of everyday life, and social scientists and social historians have begun to take into account highly articulate and imaginative expressions of culture. The emphasis on the symbolic and semiotic character of culture has also recently caused some social scientists to be directly influenced by methods of interpretation used in the humanities. As the anthropologist Clifford Geertz puts it, the analysis of culture may be viewed not as "an experimental science in search of law but an interpretive one in search of meaning": "Meaning, that elusive and ill-defined pseudoentity we were once more than content to leave philosophers and literary critics to fumble with, has now come back into the heart of our discipline. Even Marxists are quoting Cassirer; even positivists, Kenneth Burke."[7]

Referentiality vs. Figurativeness

As culture studies within the study of English is primarily concerned with analyzing the meaning that language makes, its basic approach must be a semiotic one. As a system of signs which in some way refers to our experience, language serves to evoke both something less and something more than sensory experience. On the one hand, our "word-signs" evoke less, because they are presented and perceived in a sequential fashion and can never match the immediacy and fullness of direct sensation; on the other hand they evoke something more, because they create a *linguistic* world, where words as signs combine with other words and conjure up associations that no direct sense impression need have called to mind. It is this function of language that makes interpretation inescapably part of the study of any speech or text.

No single theory of language illustrates this necessity for interpretation better than Ferdinand de Saussure's semiotic linguistics, particularly his conception of the word-sign as the embodiment of two constituents, a *signifier,* its sound-image or letter-image, and a *signified,* the concept that it serves to signify. At the same time, de Saussure emphasized that the relationship between signifier and signified is an arbitrary one. Thus, for example, the letter-image *child* in English and the letter-image *barn* in Norwegian happen to designate the same concept ("boy or girl"), whereas the identical letter-image *barn* in English and Norwegian happens to designate two different concepts ("farm building" vs. "child"). This seems to support de Saussure's main contention that each language owes its significations to its own intrinsic differential features. The prototypical illustration of this is that of phonetics; the word-sign /wi:l/ *(wheel)* does not signify anything in itself, only in terms of being phonemically different from signs like /hi:l/ *(heel)* or /si:l/ *(seal),* or /wil/ *(will)* or /wel/ *(well),* or /wi:k/ *(week)* or /wi:p/ *(weep),* and so on. In short, words mean something not primarily because they refer directly to some absolute reality "out there"; they mean something because they form a system of differential relations, the study of which demands its own methodology. This is true of semantics as well; *rain* signifies something primarily because of its differentiation from *sleet,* or *hail,* or *snow.* Although the word's semantic history must be taken into account as well, its meaning finds its particular realization in its *relationships* to other words. Such relationships may of course also be a matter of interconnections, as in the case of *rain, sleet, hail,* and *snow* having *precipitation* as a common semantic denominator.

This business of relating a word to other words is both a *syntagmatic* one, as when we link words together in speech or reading, and a *paradigmatic* one, as when words trigger off associations with other words which may not be literally present in the utterance or the text. This interplay between sequential and associative significations in language makes it impossible to argue that there is a direct, one-to-one relationship between words and their *referents* – that which some of them separately seem to designate in the world "outside" of language. The associative meanings of language are produced by the various cultural contexts in which language is being used, through which it has acquired its richness of meanings. Of course, certain significations always become historically established as conventional, dominant codes. But to think of words as having merely literal meanings – as merely "mirroring" our world – is misleading; a word must always be explained in terms of other words, which in turn must be explained by yet other words, and so on. Since language is per definition polysemous, suggestive, and associative, any text – regardless of whether it is part of culture studies, history, or literary studies – requires close analysis and explication.

"Fact" vs. "Fiction"

Literary scholars have always been acutely aware of these characteristics of language, but they have first and foremost held them to be typical of literary texts. Having on the one hand viewed literary language as non-referential and highly ambiguous, they tended on the other hand to regard everyday language as predominantly referential in its function. But, as argued in the previous chapter, the fact that lyrical poetry, for example, deliberately plays on the polysemous character of words does not make everyday language necessarily literal. If one looks at people's use of language in everyday conversation or in non-literary texts, one will discover that William Empson's *Seven Types of Ambiguity* also flourish freely outside of literature.[8] Speaking and writing are never merely a matter of reproducing meaning, it is also the process by which meaning is produced – a means of both reflecting and constructing our world at one and the same time. As Kenneth Burke puts it,

> however important to us is the tiny sliver of reality each of us has experienced firsthand, the whole overall "picture" is but a construct of our symbol systems. To meditate on this fact until one sees its full implications is much like peering over the edge of things into an ultimate abyss. And doubtless that's one reason why, though man is typically the symbol-using animal, he clings to a kind of naive verbal realism that refuses to realize the full extent of the role played by symbolicity in his notions of reality.[9]

It is in this connection that it becomes important for a text-oriented field like culture studies to abolish the conception – stubbornly held both inside and outside the humanities – that the study of imaginative literature deals with "fiction," whereas historical studies deal with "facts." A useful point of departure for demolishing this myth may be the following Doonesbury cartoon from the early 1970s, in which one American says to the other as they are trudging through a Vietnamese landscape of tall weeds: "Hear of the bombing raid last night? 2,300 tons!" – to which the other replies, "That wasn't a bombing raid! It was a Protective Reaction Strike!" This exchange illustrates two crucial aspects of language-oriented culture studies: first, that most historical facts represent problems of interpretation long before they reach history books, and secondly that they do so precisely because problems of language are always involved as well. This is not to say that we cannot talk of facts and that they do not make a difference; indeed, the exact tonnage of the above-mentioned bombs and the particular destruction they caused are matters of no mean importance on which to reach some agreement in historical studies. At the same time, however, one should be aware that facts, when they enter a historical account, inevitably become part of an interpretive context. It is not bombs that we find in written documents, but words about them.

Language inevitably seems to make man into what Roger Fowler calls "a fiction-making animal": "We understand our universe by naming its parts – or so we like to think. Of course what we really do is partition our universe fictionally by an imposed grid of language."[10] This is poignantly obvious in the expressions above, where the "bombing raid" and the "Protective Reaction Strike" conjure up, as it were, two different worlds, in both of which there are 2,300 tons of facts. One may indeed ask which world makes the facts most "fictional," or whose "fictions" are the most "factual."

In order to have some absolute existence in and by themselves, facts would have to stay outside language – the moment they enter it, they become part of a *particular* experience. They enter a specific emotional context as well; when the cartoon character above says that "they drop bombs in both cases. There's no difference," the other exclaims, "There's a *big* difference, fellah! A Protective Reaction Strike means not having to say you're sorry."[11] Thus our emotional reactions and attitudes are inextricably interwoven into the very words we use – into the web of our facts and fictions.

These observations are not meant to reduce history – in the spirit of postmodernism – to a mere matter of competing fictions. Instead, they are intended to suggest that language always has *both* a referential and a figurative dimension. It is perhaps hard to keep this double function of language constantly in mind. The only time we seem to be familiar with this referential non-referentiality, is in the case of conventional poetic metaphors. Thus, when the bride of "The Song of Solomon" says that "I am a rose of Sharon,/ a lily of the valleys," we do not mistake her for a flower; and when the bridegroom says to her that "Your lips distil nectar, my bride;/ honey and milk are under your tongue," we are not liable to think that, upon kissing her, he discovers that she has just eaten breakfast – despite the fact that rose, lily, honey, and milk are all *bona fide* references. What is true of such metaphors is also in varying degrees true of the language of an ordinary conversation, a discursive essay, or an imaginative work of fiction. Language has difficulties pinning down, so to speak, some "reality" that is one-dimensional and still; instead it constantly flickers ambiguously between that which is made and that which it makes up.

Thus, historical and cultural studies do not escape the fundamental interpretive problems inherent in linguistic representation. As the American historian Carl Becker suggested already in 1926 in a paper entitled "What Are Historical Facts?", history always involves *re-presented* events, hence something that is inescapably *emblematic* rather than merely "real" or "factual." Thus, the study of history deals only with symbols of events: "In truth the actual past is gone; and the world of history is an intangible world, re-created imaginatively, and present in our minds."[12] A passage from Becker's seminal Presidential Address to the American Historical Association in 1931 actually combines this concept of history as an "imaginative reconstruction" of the past with the idea of history as a linguistic means of expression – hence history, like literature, becomes not a reflection of some "objective" "truth," but rather a production of the subjective vision of the writer himself:

> Left to themselves, the facts do not speak; left to themselves they do not exist, not really, since for all practical purposes there is no fact until some one affirms it . . . the form and substance of historical facts, having a negotiable existence only in literary discourse, vary with the words employed to convey them. Since history is not part of the external material world, but an imaginative reconstruction of vanished events, its form and substance are inseparable: in the realm of literary discourse substance, being an idea, *is* form; and form, conveying the idea, *is* substance. It is thus not the undiscriminated fact, but the perceiving mind of the historian that speaks.[13]

The culture studies scholar should consequently avoid terminological dichotomies like fact vs. fiction, imagination vs. reality, illusion vs. truth, and so on, which traditionally have flourished in the humanities. As Gene Wise suggests in his book *American Historical Explanations,* we should perhaps talk "*not of 'reality' and of 'truth' vis-à-vis that reality, but of 'experience' and of 'explanations' vis-à-vis that experience.*"[14] Such formulations serve to bring out the interpretive frame of mind that should guide the work of both culture studies and literary studies.

The "fact-minded" historian of culture and the exclusively "fiction-minded" literary scholar may retrench, however, and dig themselves in in the last ditch by objecting that, no matter how figurative historical sources may be, I am none the less mixing up two different kinds of "fictionality" here; the symbolic-imaginative dimension of historical sources is after all of a different character from that of literary works. Be it far from me to suggest otherwise. Most of the experiences presented in historical sources, though figurative, are written or read as referring to something that has actually taken place (for instance "Protective Reaction Strikes"), whereas those of literature are usually read as make-believe. Still, as Clifford Geertz says in his cultural discussion of an account about a Jewish merchant named Cohen and his confrontations with a Berber chieftain and a French officer in Morocco in 1912, to construct their actor-oriented relations is clearly an imaginative act, not at all that different from constructing similar descriptions of, say, the involvements with one another of a provincial French doctor, his silly, adulterous wife, and her feckless lover in nineteenth century France. In the latter case, the actors are represented as not having existed and the events as not having happened, while in the former they are represented as actual, or as having been so. This is a difference of no mean importance; indeed, precisely the one Madame Bovary had difficulty grasping. But the importance does not lie in the fact that her story was created while Cohen's was only noted. The conditions of their creation, and the point of it (to say nothing of the manner and the quality) differ. But the one is as much a *fictio* – "a making" – as the other.[15]

The traditional distinction between "factual" and "fictional" accounts is therefore quite problematic and highly amorphous. Our conventions of reading often make us regard the experiences presented in literary works as being closely related to those of life; and life, we say, imitates fiction. (Inversely, we also say that fact is sometimes "stranger than fiction.") What is more, the language of "fictional" discourse is referential at the same time, and the language of everyday discourse also functions imaginatively. Again, it is crucial to emphasize that the belief in a specific "reality" is a matter of cultural conditioning; to people of one culture or sub-culture, the beliefs of radically different groups may seem quite "fictional." Unconventionally speaking, the worlds in which different social groups see themselves living are myths – their own particular versions of the world – within which there are, conventionally speaking, worlds of make-believe (like those of dreams, fables, games, or imaginative literature.)

The central point in this connection is therefore not that the fictions of literary make-believe and cultural beliefs are functionally identical. We certainly approach the analysis of fiction with a different mental set than in the case of non-fiction; this also affects our particular interpretation. What I argue, however, is that, as both historical and literary source materials are linguistic ones, they must be interpreted in related ways. Their character as linguistic means of expression inevitably imposes upon them similar interpretive problems. Thus, whether events have taken place or not is not pertinent for the *methods* by which we *semiotically* study their expression within the structure of the sources themselves. There can be no essential difference involved when it comes to our means of analyzing the "composition" they construe, the "figure" they make, the "story" they tell.

Thus the dichotomy of "fact" vs. "fiction" is in my opinion inept, unproductive, and even downright misleading, when used to characterize historical vs. literary sources and studies. Such a distinction reduces the interpretative potentiality of both disciplines, as both kinds of sources and studies are referential and imaginative at one and the same time. More than a mere squabble over terms is involved here; the disagreement marks two distinct attitudes to human studies. The "fact vs. fiction" attitude seems to imply that life can be analyzed in exclusively referential terms: that facts can be separated from values; description (information) from interpretation; thought from ideology; and "reality" from myth. In short, it reflects a belief in some sort of "objective" knowledge that is given and has some absolute ontological status. My position, on the other hand, is that life must also be analyzed in figurative terms: that facts cannot be discussed apart from our valuations; that description is at the same time interpretation; that thought is ideology; and that what we call "reality" is, semiotically speaking, a myth – a product of our own story-telling.

It is essential for scholars within the human studies to realize that substance and fantasy are intimately bound up with each other, and indeed that cultural myths, however well-founded or unfounded, help form our behavior, and vice versa. *Understanding* – whether scientific or not – is part of this process: our world is not there, apart from us, waiting to be understood; we construct it in the very act of trying to understand it. As reader-oriented critics like Stanley Fish have argued, cultural or literary knowledge is therefore not something that we merely find *"in "* texts and that lie there independently from us; it is something that we linguistically *make* in the act of reading them.[16] Thus, it is also impossible to distinguish radically between the ways in which we interpret our *beliefs* and the ways in which we interpret our *make-believe,* like literature. They are part and parcel of each other.

The Particular vs. the Representative

That our presentation of experience in this sense is always a construction, however, does not mean that it is all random, or that it cannot be studied systematically. It simply means that we have to replace an opposition like *objective vs. subjective* with oppositions like *collective vs. individual* and *representative vs. particular.* Obviously, some types of ideas and values are the collective property of a great many members of a society or a social group; these commonly held views may be analytically distinguished from those of a more individual nature. In order to disentangle the representative from the particular, the field of history is indispensable for culture studies. As any source – be it literary or historical – is in itself expressive of a single point of view, only extensive historical research can establish whether some of its assumptions may be of a cultural, which is to say widely shared, nature.

This brings us once more back to the subject of the nature of language and the question of interpretation. The most radical semiotic theories of language have tended to do away with history altogether, arguing that texts, whether literary or historical, do not refer to a world "out there"; instead, the words of any written source are regarded as signs in an autonomous linguistic system continually commenting on itself. Any historically minded critic, however, must reject this extreme position and insist on the mutual interplay and interdependence of language and culture. Thus, a culture studies approach, while paying attention to the fact that the analysis of language is always a matter of interpretation, also regards language as a historically significant, collectively shared means of *communication*. Language must not be understood only as the property of an individual text, but as the shared property of text and historical context. Thus, the language of any text becomes per definition a cultural phenomenon.

One of the most interesting historical theories of language as communication is that of M. M. Bakhtin, whose conception of the essentially *dialogic* nature of language represents an important supplement or corrective to Saussurean formalist theories. To Bakhtin, words are products of a larger context of discourse and never the sole property of the individual: "Each word tastes of the context and contexts in which it has lived its socially charged life. . . . As a living, socio-ideological concrete thing, as heteroglot opinion, language, for the individual consciousness, lies on the borderline between oneself and the other. The word in language is half someone else's."[17] The idea of words being half someone else's provides an incisive formulation of the sociocultural dimension of language uses. A culture studies approach represents precisely a way of paying attention to the dialogic relationship between language and history. Although a cultural approach to the study of any text always involves interpretation, it is an interpretation that, in its concern with the *representativeness* of the formulation of beliefs and values, serves to illustrate how historically oriented readers are never free, willy-nilly, to produce their own text. By being restricted and guided by the interplay between the text and its historical context, they must bring to their studies not only a textual-analytical competence, but also an extensive knowledge of historical and cultural analysis.

Thus, while so-called non-literary and literary sources demand similar techniques of interpretation, the cultural study of texts differs in some important ways from the manner in which literary works have traditionally been studied. Because any historical document, including literary sources, expresses only a particular view, cultural ideas are not found in them, ready-made as it were, like so many pearls on a string. The study of complex historical issues involves questions of generalization and representativeness to which no single type of source can provide a satisfactory answer. It is necessary to read a wide range of cultural sources – primary as well as secondary – before one can confidently talk of features that they may share, evaluate the respective importance of these, and interpret their significance. To use only *one* type of source – only literary ones, or nothing but newspaper reports, or exclusively diaries and letters – carries its own risk of distortion and one-sidedness. The historical crux of the matter is that the common ideological denominators we find at a particular time within one kind of source are not necessarily widely held in the culture at large; they may simply be typical of the character of this specific type of source material. Thus, we always have to make cross-checks with other kinds of source as well. In retrospect some of these sources, including literary ones, may be found indeed to be embodiments of collective and representative issues.

This kind of historical methodology, which is central to culture studies, carries us a long way away from the type of study that conventionally has characterized literary criticism. Historically oriented studies are concerned with sifting out non-representative assumptions and judgments by constantly checking sources against other sources, whereas the study of a literary work has often centered on the particular vision of the text itself. The generalizations in culture studies are often *supra*-textual ones, that is, constructions of collective issues that may not be fully present and developed in any one text; the generalizations of literary studies, however, have often remained purely *intra*-textual ones, i.e. constructions of the intrinsic characteristics of one specific text. In short, cultural and literary studies have often differed from each other in the sense that the ultimate cognitive objective of the former has been a collective or representative one, whereas the objective of the latter has tended to be an individual and particularized one. There is no reason, of course, why these supra-textual and intra-textual approaches cannot be combined – which is precisely what they should be in the cultural study of any text, whether it happens to be a so-called non-literary or a literary one.

The discipline of culture studies involves the understanding of both synchronic and diachronic contexts – that which is shared in a culture at a given point in time, and that which is the product of a particular sociohistorical development. To use an example from Chapter 4 on culture and language: when Ronald Reagan was speaking of his space program, he declared: "Our second great goal is to build on America's pioneer spirit . . . to develop . . . our next frontier: space. . . . The Space Age is barely a quarter of a century old. But already we've pushed civilization forward with our advances in science and technology."[18] Looking up the word "frontier" in a dictionary and finding it, among other meanings, to designate a border area between the wilderness and organized society, would not carry the reader very far. A knowledge of its specific American implications would be necessary, linking it to that other term of the sentence, "pioneer." In short, the first sentence semantically demands the kind of historical and cultural insight that would be provided by, say, a lecture on the settlement of America. Then, possibly, one would also catch the heavily 19th century ring to the sentences "The Space Age is barely a quarter of a century old. But already we've pushed civilization forward with our advances in science and technology." This inevitably brings to mind the 19th century American ideology of the so-called "advance" of "civilization," which justified the conquest of a whole continent and its native peoples – with all the tragic consequences of the philosophy of Manifest Destiny, of which, to be sure, Reagan did not intend his listeners to be reminded. The main import of this passage is obviously to make us think of the future conquest of space in 19th century American ideological terms. As such an example serves to demonstrate, it is the interdisciplinary combination of historical, cultural, and linguistic perspectives that makes culture studies an interpretive humanities study.

This interpretive orientation is central for the way in which textual studies have been conceptualized in this chapter. Although the discipline of culture studies is ultimately concerned with collective assumptions and values, it must insist that these can only be established on the basis of the close analysis of the particular views expressed in particular texts. As Gene Wise puts it,

> In calling a source "primary," historians are often inclined to believe that's where history *is,* in the source. . . . But a primary document is not the original experience. It may be *an* original experience – but only for the framer(s) of that document. Which means it's already filtered by the time the historian gets to it. It's not the full happening, it's someone's particular image of that happening.[19]

The ways in which an author chooses to formulate his views are therefore indicative of his individual perception of his own culture. Thus, ideas cannot be lifted separately from a textual passage without paying attention to their signification within the text as a whole – the way in which they acquire their meaning from the interplay of all the linguistic-figurative means of expression within a text. Since a text is not only an *expression of,* but also a *reaction to,* a specific period, this double signification is imbedded in the very texture of its language. The study of texts therefore requires an exacting and refined analytical approach, which can enable the reader to deal with both their creation and their reproduction of meaning.

When faced with the complexity of these issues, traditional historians or conventional cultural scholars may feel that the interpretive competence required brings them too far beyond the orthodox boundaries of their discipline. Thus, they may want to scuttle – with considerable relief – back to their "factual" studies. Yet – to return to my semiotic perspective – most of what I have tried to argue in this chapter is meant to embitter their sigh of happy relief. I have tried to suggest that all written or oral sources are imaginative constructions. As the narrator puts it in Bernard Malamud's novel *Dubin's Lives*: "The past exudes legend: one can't make pure clay out of time's mud. There is no life that can be recaptured wholly; as it was."[20] Not even sources whose languages are traditionally considered relatively "hard" are wholly exempt from this – for example those of official documents rather than personal diaries. The historically oriented student of culture pursues an illusion if she or he regards the meaning of such sources as directly "paraphrasable," that is, if he or she thinks that they simply "contain" historical "information" that can be directly "transferred" as "facts" to a historical study.

Of course, the use and perception of figurativeness may vary from source to source and from reader to reader: it may be quite deliberately practised and read as such, like *for example* in poetry ("Your lips distil nectar"); it may be partly consciously employed and understood, as in various types of political "languages" ("bombing raids" or "Protective Reaction Strikes"); or it may be by and large unconsciously presented and perceived, as often in everyday speech or in what we regularly regard as "referential language" ("2,300 tons of bombs") (cf. the difference with equally "factual" formulations like the more abstract "a bomb tonnage of 2,300," or the more plenteous "two million three hundred thousand kilos of bombs"). No source presents pure "information"; imbedded in the very language of which it is made, is always – in varying degrees – a specific figurative and normative response. A student of historical sources is at every turn confronted with things both being, and not being, referential. This inescapable ambiguity may not make the traditional, fact-oriented historian happy but – *c'est la vie*.

In order to underscore the interpretive interconnections between historical and literary studies, let me close with a small anecdote from "real life," or rather from my dream life, slightly heightened, perhaps, through poetic licence. Once I had a nightmare about taking an English oral exam on the podium of some enormous auditorium with two examiners seated before me. One of them seemed to be a professor of linguistics who kept hissing agitatedly into his microphone with an unmistakably Norwegian accent: "He's made THREE grammatical agreement errors in one hour and ten minutes! He's made THREE agreement errors in one hour and ten minutes!" The other examiner was a professor of literature in a black dress and shawl who seemed singularly unimpressed with my discussion. She was not listening any more; I knew I had not made it but continued talking. Suddenly, however, she looked up from her black knitting: "All right, then – what do you mean when you keep saying that literature is *imaginative?*" Everything grew quiet; even the linguistics professor stopped hissing. Imaginative literature... IMAGINATIVE... Finally I stuttered, to break the silence: "It is sort of... sort of like my wife. When I say, well, how I love her and all, she says that that person isn't really her." All at once the examiners and the whole auditorium burst into laughter. And then, like a silly puppet, I started laughing as well, although it felt more like crying.

Such laughter may have grown steadily more shrill in the last few decades as linguists, anthropologists, and psychologists have started to deprive us of the stability of our "facts." Our laughter is also in many ways a particularly Western one, engendered by a deep-rooted positivist tradition from which we have the greatest difficulties in freeing ourselves. Ironically, the theories of the so-called hard sciences have long since shorn the positivist chains that we keep rattling. But as long as we, historical and literary students alike, departmentalize wives or literature (or husbands or dreams or protective bombings or Huckleberry Finns or Ronald Reagans) into a world of *either* "fact" *or* "fiction," the discipline of culture studies remains at a standstill. Only by combining an interpretive semiotics with a concern for historical representativeness will culture studies escape this stalemate and come into its own as a genuinely interdisciplinary field of study.

Notes

1 Myrdal, *An American Dilemma* (New York: Harper and Row, 1962; originally published 1944), p. 1041.
2 Bateson, *Steps to an Ecology of Mind* (New York: Ballantine, 1972), p. 39.
3 Kuhn, *The Structure of Scientific Revolutions,* Second Edition (Chicago: Univ. of Chicago Press, 1970), pp. 103, 206, 171, 206. See also his chapter "Revolutions as Changes of World View," pp. 111-135.
4 Dewey's statement cited and used as a premise in Myrdal's *An American Dilemma,* p. lxxi (see note 1).
5 A.L. Kroeber and Clyde Kluckhohn, *Culture: A Critical Review of Concepts and Definitions* (New York: Vintage Books, 1963), pp. 340-341.
6 Jaeger and Selznick, "A Normative Theory of Culture," in Robert Merideth, ed., *American Studies: Essays on Theory and Method* (Columbus, Ohio: Charles E. Merrill, 1968), p. 97.
7 Geertz, "Thick Description: Toward an Interpretive Theory of Culture," *The Interpretation of Cultures* (New York: Basic Books, 1973), pp. 5, 29.
8 Empson, *Seven Types of Ambiguity* (Penguin: Harmondsworth, 1961).
9 Kenneth Burke, *Language as Symbolic Action* (Berkeley: Univ. of California Press, 1966), p. 5.
10 Roger Fowler, "The Structure of Criticism and the Languages of Poetry: An Approach through Language," in Malcolm Bradbury and David Palmer, eds., *Contemporary Criticism* (London: Edward Arnold, 1970), p. 189.

11 G.B. Trudeau, *But This War Had Such Promise* [a "Doonesbury Book"] (New York: Holt, Rinehart, and Winston, 1973), no pagination (about p. 47).
12 Becker, "What Are Historical Facts?" *Western Political Quarterly*, 8, no. 3 (September 1955), 333.
13 Becker, "Everyman His Own Historian," *American Historical Review*, 37, no. 2 (January 1932), 234-235.
14 Wise, *American Historical Explanations: A Strategy for Grounded Inquiry* (Homewood, Ill.: Dorsey Press, 1973), p. 50.
15 Geertz, "Thick Description," pp. 15-16 (see note 7).
16 See Stanley Fish, *Is There a Text in This Class?* (Cambridge, Mass.: Harvard Univ. Press, 1980). Such views are also implicit in Gregory Bateson's work, *Steps to an Ecology of Mind* (cf. note 2) and *Mind and Nature: A Necessary Unity* (New York: Bantam Books, 1979).
17 Bakhtin, *The Dialogic Imagination* (Austin: Univ. of Texas Press, 1981), p. 293.
18 Reagan, "State of the Union Address," January 25, 1984, in *Historic Documents of 1984* (Washington, D.C.: Congressional Quarterly, 1985), p. 89.
19 Wise, *American Historical Explanations*, p. 73 (see note 14).
20 Malamud, *Dubin's Lives* (New York: Avon Books, 1979), p. 20.

7
Culture and Text: Culture Studies as a Philological Discipline

As the preceding chapters on sociocultural, linguistic, literary, and historical approaches to the interpretation of culture serve to demonstrate, the text-oriented field of culture studies within the subject of English must inevitably become interdisciplinary. Such a conception of culture studies brings it near to the field of *philology* as it was traditionally pursued in the humanities before the introduction of strictly formalist studies in linguistics and literature.

The Nature of Philology

In philology, the studies of culture, history, language, and literature were considered part and parcel of each other. In the study of older texts, situated in a different rhetorical tradition from modern ones, there were no sharp divisions drawn between imaginative literature and other kinds of text. It was in the 18th and 19th centuries and later that terms like "artist" and "literature" were severed from the more general concepts of "artisan" and "writing" and thus came to signify something exclusive and élitist.[1]

Broadly defined, the field of philology in the 19th and early 20th centuries involved the general study of linguistic, cultural, and intellectual history on the basis of a great variety of imaginative and more prosaic texts. More narrowly defined, however, philology has to the present day been a matter of reconstructing old source material, for example Old English or Old Norse texts, in cases where doubt about their authenticity existed, for instance where several versions of the same text were found. On the basis of a meticulous analysis of extensive linguistic, cultural, and literary evidence, the philologist has attempted to (re)establish the most plausible and "correct" text.

Of course, this problem of textual reconstruction does not exist with modern, printed texts; thus, a narrowly defined philological approach would seem superfluous. Yet, as recent semiotic and reader-oriented theories of language and literature serve to demonstrate, it is only through the act of reading that a text acquires meaning and significance. According to this mode of thinking, a text is never given; it is always and unceasingly constructed anew. This modern view of textual interpretation once more actualizes the relevance of a philological approach to the analysis of texts. In particular the field of foreign language study seems to lend itself naturally to the interdisciplinary perspective of philology, in terms of which the subdisciplines of literary study, linguistics, and culture studies may, ultimately at least, serve to elucidate each other and thus create a comprehensive analytical framework for the interpretation of the language of texts.

Philological interpretation, however, is always caught in a dilemma: on the one hand, it attempts to demonstrate how a text linguistically constructs a particular cultural vision of the world; on the other hand, this demonstration is in itself the product of the interpreter's own construction. The tension between these two interpretive levels makes text-oriented culture studies a very precarious affair. Any interpretation must attempt to be sensitive to the nuances and complexities of language and let the text speak, as it were, for itself – in the voice of its own time and culture. Yet it cannot ultimately speak for itself, and a humanities scholar must avoid creating the illusion that the study of language is merely a matter of reproducing some textual-cultural meaning. The problem is particularly acute when one studies a foreign language and culture: on the one hand, by expressing one's own particular view of a text, one runs the danger of forcing the text, of imposing one's own (perhaps ethnocentric) ideas on it; on the other hand, by trying to avoid explicitly interpretive judgments, one runs the danger of creating the illusion of objectivity, of implying that the message of the text is intrinsically "given."

A Philological Analysis of a Text

Let me illustrate these textual-interpretive problems by analyzing two passages from a speech by President Ronald Reagan. It is not a text that I would present to novice students of American life. A considerable amount of knowledge of American history and culture is required to grasp the full implications of the few brief paragraphs below. Students should probably be given a text like this for analysis only towards the end of their first year course in American culture studies. It is a good example, however, of how knowledge of English grammar would only bring them halfway there. A foreign reader with no acquaintance with American history and culture would miss the semantic webs woven by the words and phrases in this speech.

The objective of my philological analysis is twofold: to show how Reagan's speech brings to mind a series of dominant American belief patterns embodying a particular cultural vision; and at the same time to formulate this so as to explicitly express my own – an individual reader's – particular view of the text. The two excerpted passages are from Reagan's 1986 State of the Union Address to Congress:

> But, it wasn't long ago that we looked out on a different land – locked factory gates, long gasoline lines, intolerable prices and interest rates turning the greatest country on earth into a land of broken dreams. Government growing beyond our consent had become a lumbering giant, slamming shut the gates of opportunity, threatening to crush the very roots of our freedom.
> What brought America back? The American people brought us back – with quiet courage and common sense; *[applause]* with undying faith that in this nation under God the future will be ours, for the future belongs to the free.
> Tonight the American people deserve our thanks – for 37 straight months of economic growth . . .
>
> -----
>
> And despite the pressures of our modern world, family and community remain the moral core of our society, guardians of our values and hopes for the future. Family and community are the costars of this Great American Comeback. They are why we say tonight: Private values must be at the heart of public policies.
> For what is true for families in America is true for America in the family of free nations. History is no captive of some inevitable force. History is made by men and women of vision and courage. Tonight, freedom is on the march. The United States is the economic miracle, the model to which the world once again turns . . . [2]

Reagan's speech is a good example of the text-as-intertext; it contains fragments of the language of the Bible as well as of hallowed documents of American history. Metaphors like "land of broken dreams," "slamming shut the gates" of opportunity, and "crush the very roots" of freedom have an Old Testament ring to them. And, when Reagan speaks of "this nation under God," he evokes documents like The Pledge of Allegiance as well as Lincoln's Gettysburg Address, and when he talks of "Government growing beyond our consent . . ." he alludes to the Declaration of Independence. These are prominent phrases that most Americans have internalized and which consequently ought to be familiar also to the philological student of American cultural history.

Above all, however, the phrases and ideas of Reagan's address conjure up a grammar of culture that many Americans know by heart, so to speak. The images that he employs cluster around certain core beliefs and values: those of *Manifest Destiny, faith, dream, freedom, individualism,* and *progress.* Reagan's reference to the United States as "the greatest country on Earth" may seem like pure ethnocentrism to the non-American, but it is at the same time a present-day reiteration of the idea of Manifest Destiny – the belief historically ingrained in American culture that America was to establish itself as an ideal society, a Puritan city on the hill, predestined to become a Garden of Eden in a moral as well as an economic sense. Reagan's insistence that "the future" belongs to the United States thus expresses what many Americans would expect and want to hear.

Reagan's constant use of sacred and transcendental imagery functions as an appropriate extension of this theme. It is important to be aware that such imagery does not merely represent gestures of religious tokenism from a President seeking political support for his measures. It may certainly be that *as well,* but it is at the same time an evocation of a kind of cultural-religious communion: Americans are said to have an "undying faith"; the United States is seen as "a land of dreams" and associated with "men and women of vision"; and it is viewed as an economic "miracle." In this manner, culture is affirmed in an almost religious spirit. It should be emphasized that such a rhetoric could have been used by almost any American President, regardless of his political leanings. This sort of cultural "dream" imagery is also very much at the heart of literary works such as Fitzgerald's *The Great Gatsby* and Miller's *Death of a Salesman,* not to mention a text like Martin Luther King's 1964 address "I Have a Dream."

Reagan takes advantage of a firmly established American cultural grammar when he links this transcendental faith with the ideas of freedom and individualism. The words "free" or "freedom" are used no less than four times in this brief excerpt. The concept of freedom is also indirectly evoked by way of the reference to the "gates of opportunity" earlier slammed shut, referring to the creed of equality of opportunity, which should not be confused, of course, with the idea of some absolute equality. Instead, freedom is synonymous with individualism, that which Reagan links to the "private values" of "family and community." "Community" has in this context a local ring to it and is not meant to be connected with society in general. The crucial point here is that Reagan regards family values as inherently moral and at odds with something more impersonal that he calls "the pressures of the modern world." Whereas a European would more often regard such pressures as being rooted in the economic character of modern society and thus situated within the lifestyle of the families themselves, Reagan sees such modern pressures as extrinsic and connected with public – particularly "governmental" – interference in private lives.

The most striking expression of the ethos of individualism in this address is Reagan's programmatic declaration: "Private values must be at the heart of public policies." This conception of the private and the public is not restricted to conservatives only; it is a phenomenon of a general cultural character. A great many Americans regard private values as primary and per definition positive. People of many other cultures, however, may be less convinced of this, and may argue that public policies are sometimes more genuinely community-oriented than those dictated by private interests. To many Scandinavians, for example, the inverse statement may have seemed equally appropriate for the idea of *communitas:* "Public values must be at the heart of private policies."

In the context of Reagan's rhetoric, however, it seems only appropriate that he should round off his public celebration of individualism with an anti-Communist decree: "History is no captive of some inevitable force. History is made by men and women of vision and courage." This reflects the conventional conception of history as a product of the acts of extraordinary individuals rather than of the social life of people at large. The idea of *making* history turns it into a form of personal action and makes it a future-oriented rather than a past-oriented affair. There is something typically American about this propensity for, as it were, individualizing history. Reagan speaks within a long American tradition in this respect; Ralph Waldo Emerson, for example, suggested in his essay "Self-Reliance" that "The man must be so much that he must make all circumstance indifferent. Every true man is a cause, a country, and an age . . . all of history resolves itself very easily into the biography of a few stout and earnest persons."[3]

These five paragraphs by Reagan present a kind of plot, a narrative, of success. It starts with the land of broken dreams, proceeds by way of reference to the recovery created by people's "quiet courage" and by family and community, and ends with the vision of an economic miracle. The central implications of this success story are evoked by words like "comeback," "future," "great," "growth," and "on the march." The use of the word "comeback" seems quite appropriate coming from a former actor; it is also befitting a conservative President who continually argued that America should revive her traditional capitalist value system. Reagan's come<u>back</u> was of course seen as <u>back</u>lash by his political opponents, but Reagan here links it with the word "future," which is repeated three times in two paragraphs. In American culture this future-oriented idea of progress is quite often equated with capitalist expansion pure and simple. It is rather typical that Reagan directly combines freedom and finance in the following two sentences: "Tonight, freedom is on the march. The United States is the economic miracle . . ." In this manner, freedom becomes analogous with economic growth. This vision of freedom-as-expansiveness is also evoked by the repetition of the idiom "great" (with its connotations of size and magnitude), as well as by the expression "on the march" (with its military connotations). Thus, success and progress are seen as synonymous with mobility. By his reiteration of such views, Reagan affiliates himself with dominant belief patterns in American culture.

The main intention of an analysis like this one, however, has been to show that language and culture are intertwined, and that understanding of one requires knowledge of the other. One tends to notice what one is predisposed to seeing; Reagan's speech would merely seem like inflated rhetoric to somebody only acquainted, say, with Norwegian political culture. His address requires a familiarity with the whole web of cultural connotations spun from the American core values of individualism and personal freedom – in particular the way in which many Americans (like Reagan above) tend to invest these ideas with a transcendental fervor that turns it all into something akin to a religious faith. If one fails to grasp this point, one may fail to take an excerpt such as this one seriously, which is not the best starting point for cultural communication, for acquiring a *communicative competence* – the ultimate aim of any language teaching.

Thus, I believe that this analysis of Reagan's speech represents one way of contributing towards the acquisition of such a competence. As an example of a cultural-philological approach to textual analysis, it may in a small way serve, as Clifford Geertz says about ethnographic accounts, "to clarify what goes on in such [faraway] places, to reduce the puzzlement – what manner of men are these?"[4] Of course, my interpretation of Reagan's text embodies a critical perspective, reflected for example in the comparisons between European and American attitudes towards individualism and in the passing remark on the word "comeback" (as an appropriate use of language for a former actor-turned-conservative). Such critical comments, however, are based on the explication of the language of the text itself, and are therefore not, as in the case of ethnocentric views, imposed on it. In fact, I do not believe that critical reflections, when explicit, make textual analysis less valuable or representative – quite the contrary. Particularly within the fields of the humanities, intellectual honesty requires that interpretation be made explicit rather than implicit, and value judgments overt rather than covert.

Some Reservations About Cultural Generalizations

Other problems are involved in the cultural analysis of texts, however, which the interpretation above does not escape. However representative some cultural beliefs are, and however much generalizations about them are qualified by phrases like "for many Americans . . ." or "in some ways, American culture is . . ." etc., one is inevitably left with the feeling that one constructs too much, and leaves out too much in the process. The analysis of dominant assumptions may all too easily lead to cultural heterogeneity being ignored. And even when the discussion is confined to major culture patterns, one's analysis of them may inevitably fail to catch their diversity and complexity. As Clifford Geertz puts it,

> Cultural analysis is intrinsically incomplete. And, worse than that, the more deeply it goes the less complete it is. It is a strange science whose most telling assertions are its most tremulously based, in which to get somewhere with the matter at hand is to intensify the suspicion, both your own and that of others, that you are not quite getting it right.[5]

This is a feeling one tends to have not only in cultural analysis, but in the interpretation of works of imaginative literature as well. The moment one launches into major interpretive generalizations about a text, one has the feeling that something crucial in the diversity of that work is immediately lost. Indeed, one is tempted to suggest that all philological construction involves this particular problem. In my own work with a text-oriented culture studies, I have not found a solution to this dilemma, and probably there is none.

In order to counteract this effect of cultural generalization, however, one may try to make one's interpretive uncertainties in culture studies explicit. If a cultural analysis — like the one of Reagan's speech above — fails to have incorporated into itself the interpreter's own irksome misgivings, then it becomes necessary to self-reflexively introduce these doubts. And, to return to the subject of Reagan's address, I have a nagging feeling that my own construction, though verifiable and instructive, none the less calls for some supplement. One problem is that my analysis remains an almost exclusively intrinsic one. What it obviously has failed to emphasize is that Reagan's speech is situated within a specific sociocultural context and represents a strategy by which Reagan rhetorically manages to identify a highly generalized version of Americanism with his particular, conservative policies, so as to promote these policies to the members of Congress and the public who do not necessarily agree with them. While his ideological formulations are so general as to be almost culturally incontestable, this is not true of the use to which they are put. The cultural *function* of Reagan's speech is therefore more complex than I have been able to show.

Another reason why my interpretive construction does not quite get the matter right is that it fails to incorporate a sense of diversity into its generalizations about American culture. My assertion that "a great many Americans" would publicly subscribe to Reagan's ideological formulations is not incorrect so much as it is incomplete. I am bothered, somehow, by leaving the matter of the world view of "a great many Americans" here. The fact that people may identify with certain general postulates does not mean that they do not hold other, different, and even conflicting views as well. A case in point is many of the opinion polls conducted during Reagan's Presidency: while a great majority found his general ideology appealing, they were very much divided on the subject of *particular* policies and programs. This indicates that there are some fundamental contradictions at work in American culture, which for obvious reasons are not included in Reagan's address. Thus, the analysis of a speech like this must be supplemented by the close study of other types of text from different sociopolitical contexts, which would uncover other attitudes to the free enterprise society than those Reagan eulogizes in his speech. Even the language of the *Esquire* text quoted in Chapter 5 – with its profile of the President of the American Express Company – evinced, on closer analysis, quite ambivalent ideas about American *laissez-faire* economics. Furthermore, however representative these additional beliefs may be, they are once again only particular interpretive constructions, which in turn may be supplemented by yet other assumptions.

In sum, although I believe my reading of Reagan's speech to be defensible as well as useful for its delineation of the American ideas of Manifest Destiny, freedom, and individualism, such generalizations about a particular culture inevitably seem to invite qualifications, which may produce new generalizations, which in turn may give rise to yet other reservations, and so it goes on. There is no ultimate rock bottom in culture studies. Once again, Clifford Geertz expresses the problem of cultural interpretation succinctly – and metaphorically – in terms of a tale that itself is pure metaphor: "There is an Indian story – at least I heard it as an Indian story – about an Englishman who, having been told that the world rested on a platform which rested on the back of an elephant which rested in turn on the back of a turtle, asked . . . what did the turtle rest on? Another turtle. And that turtle? 'Ah, Sahib, after that it is turtles all the way down.'"[6]

Notes

1. For an incisive discussion of the sociocultural development of these and other related terms, see Raymond Williams, *Culture and Society* (London: Chatto & Windus, 1958), pp. 30-48, particularly 43-44.
2. Reagan's "State of the Union Address," *Congressional Quarterly*, Febr. 8, 1986, p. 273.
3. Emerson, "Self-Reliance," *The Selected Writings of Ralph Waldo Emerson*, ed. Brooks Atkinson (New York: Modern Library, 1950), p. 154.
4. Clifford Geertz, "Thick Description: Toward an Interpretive Theory of Culture," *The Interpretation of Cultures* (New York: Basic Books, 1973), p. 16.
5. Geertz, "Thick Description," p. 29.
6. Geertz, "Thick Description," pp. 28-29.

8
Culture and the Class-room: Culture Studies as a Didactic Discipline

For more than twenty years now, the discipline of culture studies has been a third partner to the studies of literature and linguistics within the field of English at many Scandinavian universities and colleges. So far, however, we have not reached a general consensus on how to teach it. In their thinking around this issue, many culture studies teachers are quite naturally drawn to the work within "British Studies" and "American Studies" in the United Kingdom and the United States. It is important to stress, however, that English departments in foreign countries occupy a disciplinary position fundamentally different from that of similar institutions in Britain or America. Because we teach English to *non-native* students, our teaching of the discipline of culture studies must be subordinated to the overall aim of foreign language learning. Two crucial pragmatic questions then spring to mind: What sort of analytical procedure should we pursue in our teaching of culture studies? And what sort of cultural material should our students of English have as the object of study in order to best promote the learning and understanding of that language?

In our teaching of British or American culture to first year university and college students, we often become exasperated at the numerous disciplines and the almost unlimited amount of material that seem pertinent to our course. But much of the information on Britain and America, however interesting it is in its own right, is more or less irrelevant to language teaching. Of course, our students must know something about, say, the geographical, social, and political characteristics of the United Kingdom and the United States, but whether Colorado is north or south of Wyoming, whether poverty in America at the moment is calculated to be 12.5% or 13.8%, or whether a majority of Irish-Americans voted for President Bush in the last election, are surely not issues that necessarily contribute to the learning of English. And, although it is important for us as teachers to be abreast of recent developments in the United States or the United Kingdom, it is an open question whether our students should be bombarded with large amounts of sociological or political information. Language, thank goodness, tends to change considerably more slowly than sociopolitical issues, and we should worry a little less, perhaps, about how up-to-date our students are, and worry a little more about how we, as language teachers, should deal with the study of British and American culture – what it is, precisely, that we want our students to learn.

Four Pitfalls of the Teaching of Culture Studies

In my opinion, there are at least four main ways in which we as culture studies teachers have been diverted from our central tasks as scholars of English. The first pitfall into which we have often fallen is what I would term the *institutions syndrome* (Figure 1), where an inordinate amount of the teaching concerns itself with various institutions of the United Kingdom and the United States, particularly the political ones. Thus we end up overwhelming the students with political information.

Figure 1. The Institutions Syndrome

It is important not to be misunderstood on this point. Of course institutions ought to be taught. Of course our students ought to acquire some familiarity with the basic organization and principles of the American and British systems of government. In my opinion, however, the subject of politics and institutions has traditionally occupied far too large a part of the culture studies syllabus – in Norway sometimes as much as a quarter of the course, which is out of all proportion to its function as part of the study of the English language. It is an open question whether, for example, a detailed knowledge of the ways in which a bill becomes a law contributes significantly to the student's understanding of English. Everyday discourse is an inclusive affair in which political terms and subject matter after all play a minor role. Why, then, make them occupy a central position in the learning of English?

The second pitfall in our teaching of British and American culture consists in our being carried away, as it were, by a preoccupation with facts and figures. This represents what I would like to call the *excess information syndrome* (Figure 2), where the students become bombarded with great amounts of sociological information.

Figure 2. The Excess Information Syndrome

This preoccupation with data is a pitfall into which we easily fall when we first teach American or British culture; one piece of information leads to another, and one interesting statistical table leads to another even more fascinating one – and before we know it we are no longer teachers of the English language but a kind of amateur demographer and sociologist, burdening our students with all kinds of statistical information.

A third pitfall into which we tend to fall in our teaching of culture studies may be named the *social engineering syndrome* (Figure 3), where we time and again end up paying a lot of attention to how social problems in Britain or America may or may not be solved.

Figure 3. The Social Engineering Syndrome

It is doubtful whether it ought to be one of our primary analytical tasks to have our students deal with British or American society in such a fashion. Social problems certainly deserve a place in our study of culture and tend to engender considerable interest, but the complex issue of their solution cannot become a central concern; we are not social planners, we are teachers of English.

The fourth major pitfall in our teaching of culture represents what I perhaps could call the *minority syndrome* (Figure 4), where almost more time appears to be spent on discussing the problems of various British or American minority groups than on analyzing the mainstream culture.

Figure 4. The Minority Syndrome

This preoccupation with minorities tends to make the ordinary middle-class American nearly disappear from view. It is pedagogically tempting, however, to spend a lot of time teaching about minority groups in particular because their problems are often quite manifest and their culture often quite different from our own (Scandinavian) culture. Another reason for focusing on minorities may be that a lot of teaching material is available on "problem areas," whereas teaching material on everyday, middle America or Britain is more scarce. It is not my intention to suggest that we should not teach the subject of minorities in Britain or America. Of course we should select one or two groups for closer exemplary study in our culture studies course. Minorities have been taught in American culture studies in Scandinavia from the very beginning in order to emphasize the heterogeneity and diversity of the culture of the United States. This is a trend that has also become marked in the U.S. in recent years. In order to rectify the traditional neglect of those groups who were not white, Anglo-Saxon, and male, scholars have, as Elizabeth Fox-Genovese puts it, "succeeded in imaginatively reclaiming the voices, representations, productions, and values of the oppressed and excluded, and they have demonstrated the cultural strength and richness of those who have been ignored."[1]

When we deal with the subject of minorities in the study of English, however, their history and present situation may be taught so as to elucidate important aspects of the *dominant* culture at the same time. After all, middle class, mainstream America does not only carry economic and political clout; it also wields considerable influence in shaping culture patterns, including those of the minorities. There has been a tendency in American Studies over the last decade to question whether American culture can be studied as a whole at all. This book, however, is based upon the supposition that there *is* something that must be characterized as a mainstream culture in the United States, the study of which may illuminate the processes of sociocultural domination and subordination in American life. To reject this perspective is, as Elizabeth Fox-Genovese puts it, "to abandon the attempt to understand the ways in which African-Americans, women, and others related to each other and, especially, to those who wielded cultural as well as social and political power. It is, in effect, to lose the national dimension of the American in American Studies."[2] Thus, to study a minority culture in relation to the dominant culture may serve to reveal how the former defines itself in terms of its relations to the latter. This does not mean that the people of a subculture accept all the value systems of the mainstream; it merely means that their discourse is inevitably shaped by their interaction with the hegemonic culture. In the study of a minority culture, one may thus show how its subcultural features are products of its adoption of, as well as reaction to, the mainstream beliefs and values.

There are other ways, however, in which a minority perspective could be introduced. When we are teaching some area of American life – the workings of the American party system, say, or the nature of American televison – we could round off the subject by examining it in relation to one specific group, for example the African Americans in the United States. To use one minority group as a recurrent motif in several subject areas may furnish an interesting inroad to the discussion of both the dominant culture and the subculture, and may test American beliefs and values in an area where, so to speak, the stress is great. It may also clarify the function of cultural dominance and hierarchy as well as sharpen awareness of cultural heterogeneity.

A more radical approach to culture studies would be to build the whole course for first year university and college students around one specific minority's relations to the dominant culture. One could study the ways in which, for example, the history and present-day situation of Native Americans have been linked to the white, Anglo-Saxon hegemony and power structure, and thus bring out the ideology implicit in the conquest of the American continent, the economic expansion, the function of the government (including the courts), the role of ethnicity and religion, and so on. It requires considerable knowledge and pedagogical experience, however, to treat both the dominant and the subcultural sides with equal historical understanding. The risk of submitting to what I have termed the *minority syndrome* in a general introduction to American culture becomes much greater when one concentrates on only one group. Thus, to analyze everything in terms of a minority's situation would probably be more appropriate for courses at the intermediate (upper division) or graduate levels of English. The main point in this connection is none the less that *any* area of American life may serve as an inroad to the analysis of prevalent American culture patterns. A particular subject is taught not only for its own sake but also for what it reveals about the character of American culture in general. The most pressing issue in culture studies is therefore not so much what *subjects* to teach as what kind of *procedure* one should pursue in cultural analysis.

The problem of the four pitfalls discussed above was precisely that they led away from the central task of general *cultural* study. Together, the pitfalls reflect to some extent the history of the teaching of civilization in Norway so far. In the beginning it involved little more than giving an introduction to the political institutions of the United Kingdom and the United States. This *institutions syndrome* has in fact proved the most persistent of them all. The next stage of culture studies within the study of English was one in which the university teachers of the discipline seemed to strive to become a sort of social scientists, leading to the emergence of what I have referred to as the *excess information syndrome* and the *social engineering syndrome*. The most recent pitfall, that of the *minority syndrome,* has, in its more extreme form, been more of a high school than a university phenomenon in Norway, and seems now to be somewhat on the wane.

It is important that my preoccupation with these syndromes is not misinterpreted. Of course we, as teachers of culture, also make use of the information and insights produced by historians, demographers, sociologists, and others. My point is simply that we must work such knowledge into our own cognitive framework, which is a philological one, not one of history or sociology. As language proficiency is a matter not only of grammatical but also of cultural competence, the focal point of our culture studies must be – as argued in Chapters 3 and 4 – the belief systems that help determine people's uses of language. It is the delineation of this general cultural "grammar" of the basic assumptions and values of a society that must be the primary objective of British and American culture studies. Thus, for example, when we teach the subject of political institutions, we are particularly concerned with the ideology imbedded in the British or American system of government, and when we deal with the economic system and the social structure of Britain or America, we ultimately focus on the system of ideas that underlies and serves to justify the economic and social life of either country. Such an approach leads us most directly to our main concern, the interdependence of language and culture.

The Interrelations of Culture, Language, and Literature

The crucial issue in foreign language teaching is thus how culture studies can be related to the two other subdisciplines of English – linguistics and literary study. The relationship between culture, language, and literature may be illustrated as in Figure 5.

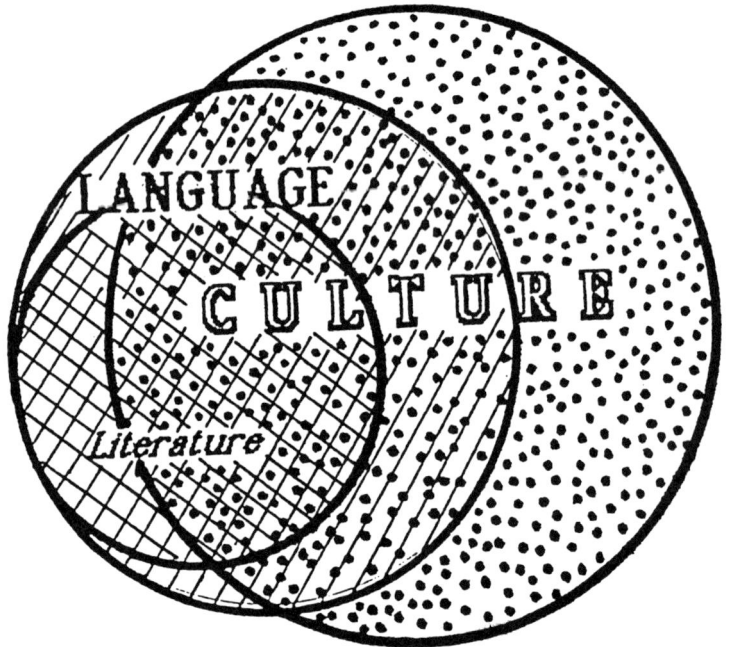

Figure 5. Culture, Language, Literature

This graphic illustration serves to reveal that language, literature, and culture are interdependent. It also shows, however, that there are dimensions of culture that fall outside the domain of language and vice versa. Of course symbolic forms other than that of language exist, which give expression to general assumptions and values – for example gestures, clothes, rituals, and artifacts.

Parenthetically it should be mentioned here that the study of non-linguistic forms of culture ought to be included in the discipline of culture studies. It is obvious that these forms cannot assume a central role within the study of English, as the use and understanding of language assumes priority. Even in their first year course, however, students ought to have at least one session on one of the arts in the United States, for example painting, photography, architecture, or music. A subject within material culture could also be of interest in this connection. Obviously such studies would help engender an awareness of the interconnections between writing (non-literary as well as literary) and other symbolic forms in the history of American culture.

Figure 5 is also meant to demonstrate that not all the uses of language fall within the domain of culture. Whether used in or outside literature, language is sometimes of such an individual or idiosyncratic character that it cannot be said to reflect dominant cultural assumptions. When the Danish-Norwegian writer Aksel Sandemose says in one of his essays that "There once was a man who blushed when he said Thursday,"[3] that man's conception of Thursday is obviously one that is not generally shared. The same can be said to be true of the Chomskyan sentence "colorless green ideas sleep furiously"[4]; it could have been a line from some kind of visionary-symbolic poetry, but not normally a verbal act in everyday discourse. This passing reference to poetry may serve to remind us that literary works, though they make use of the material of cultural discourse, often attempt to resist or subvert it by unconventional literary-stylistic strategies of their own; our teaching of literature must consequently deal with the way in which literature represents both an expression of, and a reaction and resistance to, culture.

Whether we deal with the discipline of literature or culture studies, however, our main focus in the study of English must always be that of language:

culture
↓
LANGUAGE
↑
literature

A reason why the name *culture studies* is particularly appropriate for our discipline is that it also serves to evoke our role and competence as humanities scholars and philologists. Although our non-élitist conception of *culture* as everyday belief patterns is inspired by the social sciences, the term suggests at the same time – more directly than the word *civilization* – that we are primarily concerned with *symbolic* phenomena that require interpretation, such as those of signs, artifacts, or texts. It implies that we are students of symbolic systems like that of language, the main system of signs by which we give our lives meaning. The term *culture* consequently brings us most directly back to the objective with which we started, namely, our work as language teachers.

The Use of Text in Teaching

At this point it may be useful to turn for a moment from such general, theoretical reflections to the consideration of more concrete examples. Let me use an illustration from my own teaching of how *civilization* – amorphously (non)defined – so easily carries one away into the aforementioned pitfall of the *excess information syndrome*. When teaching the subject of "Women in America" as part of the one-year civilization course in my first few years at the University of Tromsø, I presented my first term students of English with a rather comprehensive history of American women from the Puritan times to the present, including the role of women in the westward expansion and in the South; the Seneca Falls Declaration on Women's Rights and Sentiments of 1848; the part played by women in the abolitionist movement and the Civil War; the situation of middle-class and working-class women in the Gilded Age and the Progressive Era; the role of women leaders in the same period; the struggle for the 19th Amendment to the Constitution; the Women's Liberation movements of the 1960s and 70s; and the situation of women in the United States of today, ending with a one-hour group discusssion of the political conflicts at that time around the state ratifications – or non-ratifications – of the Equal Rights Amendment. All of these issues were of course interesting to discuss, but were they actually the most appropriate ones, given the fact that they were part of the teaching of English, and not part of some history course? Would it not have been a good idea, given the priorities of an already packed English study, to spend a little less time on historical information, and a little more time on, for example, cultural beliefs about the role of women and men in the United States of today? Why not use a group session to make the students discuss these assumptions about men and women? And why not use a text or two as the starting point for such a discussion? One could, for example, have started the group session off by using the following text from an advertisement for women's underwear, the Maidenform "Sweet Nothings," where three pictures of a young woman – on her bed in her lingerie, in front of her dressing-table, and in a romantic setting with a handsome man – are accompanied by these lines:

**Put on
Maidenform
Sweet Nothings.
Then Dare
to Dream!**

*Sweet Nothings
are feminine, exquisite,
delicate, enchanting,
lacy and lovely.
In short, Sweet Nothings
are quite something.
Just like the dreams
they inspire.*[5]

A text like this returns us to the question of language as well as culture. One could for example ask one's students whether any of the words used above – "exquisite," "delicate," "enchanting," and "lovely" – could have been used in an advertisement for men's underwear. If not, then why not? What words could possibly be used to advertise men's briefs? "Strong?" "Durable yet elegant"? "Tough," perhaps, which would combine material with ideological characteristics? Could the emphasis on dreaming have been introduced in male-oriented advertisements for underwear as well? What cultural attitudes and assumptions do such uses of language reflect? What are some of the sociohistorical explanations of gender-marked language such as this? Indeed, one of the pedagogical gains in introducing a text like this is that it so clearly shows how language actually serves to *construct* the meaning of feminine and, inversely, masculine. Such a text also makes the students aware of the fact that many "American" patterns of beliefs are cross-cultural ones, shared by many Western cultures. (Yet, by comparing samples of advertisements for women's lingerie in Scandinavia and the United States, one can also demonstrate interesting cultural differences with regard to dominant Scandinavian and American images of femininity.)

There are several advantages in using such a short text for analysis. First, it requires less extensive knowledge of hard historical and sociological facts and thus makes group discussion easier for the student. Secondly, such a text does not represent some statement *about* culture, it is itself a primary cultural text – one which the students *themselves* make into an object for cultural analysis. And thirdly, the text makes the students discover how certain prominent cultural assumptions and values are imbedded in the very choice of words and idioms. In this manner, the use of close analysis of short texts reveals how people's language constructs a particular world in which they see themselves to be living. The field of textual culture studies thus helps abolish the idea that language presents us with information pure and simple; instead, it demonstrates how language creates a world of discourse which, in order to be understood, in turn requires a cultural competence in the reader or listener. A text like the one above thus enables us to deal directly with the relationship between speech and culture – with the learning of English.

It should be emphasized that the texts used for close analysis ought to be very short ones. Longer texts may be highly useful as supplements to the teaching of historical or social issues. As "secondary" texts, however – as texts *about* British or American society – they are inevitably read in a manner very different from that in which "primary" cultural texts are read. Brevity is a great virtue when texts are analyzed for the way in which their language expresses cultural values. The study of long essays tends to turn the students' attention away from language to general arguments and ethical discussions. Thus, the texts used for close analysis should be between half a page and two pages long, only in rare cases somewhat longer. In their culture studies course, students ought to have an anthology of very short texts, which could be directly linked to the various cultural topics for discussion. To my knowledge, such an introductory undergraduate anthology of brief, non-literary, primary texts for the foreign language teaching of culture has not yet been produced – at least not in Scandinavia. It ought to be a central task for culture studies teachers of English to compile one. The close analysis of short texts demands a great deal of hard intellectual work from the students, but as language is the main means by which cultural identity is expressed, we should not shirk the task of making students able to analyze it in non-literary texts as well.

The Three-Step Methodology of Culture Studies Teaching

Culture studies may be said to embody three main constituents, which naturally lend themselves to the three-step analytical procedure shown in Figure 6:

Figure 6. The Three Steps of Culture Studies

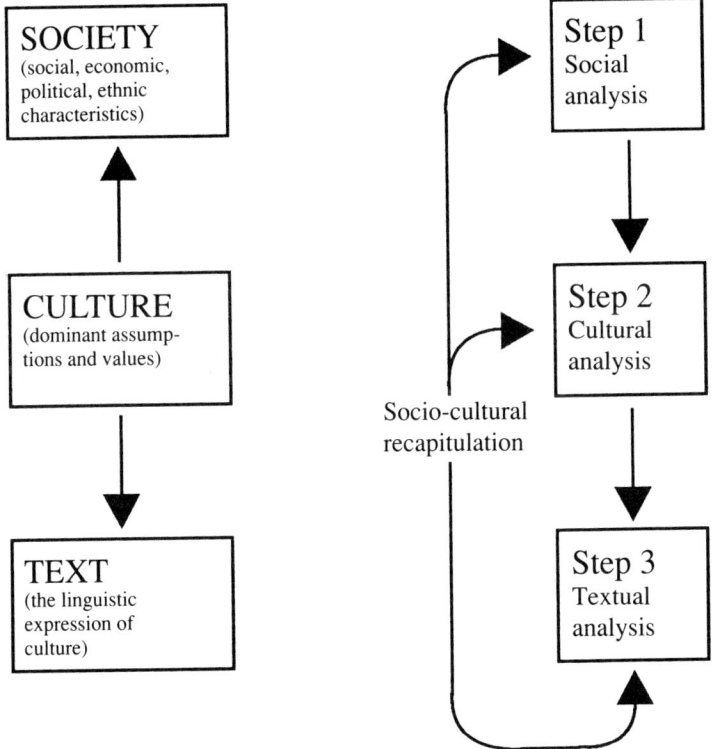

The arrows linking the CULTURE box on the *left-hand side* of this chart with the two other topical boxes of SOCIETY and TEXT mark the cognitive focus and direction of culture studies; it is the subject of *culture* that guides our choice of social and historical topics as well as our selection of texts. Sociohistorical subjects are chosen for the way in which they throw light on certain ideological conflicts, and texts are selected according to how well they give expression to such conflicting belief systems. The intention here is not to turn Marxism on its head and suggest that the superstructure precedes the base. It is merely a way of indicating that the study of the dominant patterns of assumptions and values in a society must have priority in language-oriented culture studies.

The arrows linking the analytical steps specified on the *right-hand side* of the chart, however, mark the order in which it is natural to

8 – Culture, Language,...

present these in class: first *social analysis;* then *cultural analysis;* and then *textual analysis*. STEP 1, that of social analysis, is intended to provide a general informational framework about different areas of British or American society. Belief systems cannot be discussed in a vacuum. They are shaped by economic, social, and political circumstances, and any study of culture must give a brief introduction to these. Novice foreign students of English are often surprisingly unfamiliar with British and American life, and cultural study inevitably presupposes a certain amount of hard-core knowledge. Because the present can only be fully understood in terms of past developments, this requires a certain historical perspective as well. In this connection, students should be required to read one or two general textbooks on American society (similarly on British society); a short and condensed historical introduction to, for example, its regions, social structure, economic system, ethnic make-up, religions, system of education, and government/politics, as well as to topics like mass media and popular culture. In class lectures these are discussed and developed further, preparing the ground for the discussion of culture.

But, as the main objective of such a sociohistorical introduction to the United Kingdom or the United States is to provide a factual foundation for cultural interpretation, it must be reasonably delimited. STEP 2 is then that of cultural analysis, the study of how some aspect of American life – its economic system, its class structure, or whatever – involves particular patterns of dominant assumptions and values which serve to define and legitimize it. In a procedure like this, certain basic beliefs will obviously be found to recur in different subject areas. These are the basic constituents of an American view of life and include particular notions of freedom, equality, and the pursuit of happiness, which may be further particularized by way of ideological dichotomies such as civil equality vs. socio-economic inequality, free enterprise vs. monopoly capitalism, individualism vs. conformity, production vs. consumption, hard work vs. leisure, self-denial vs. self-gratification, self-assertion vs. popularity, and uniformity vs. diversity – to mention a few dominant ones. These ideological cornerstones of American life could, of course, have been taught separately as subjects in themselves, but that would make culture studies into a rather abstract and free-floating history of ideas. It is much better to let these ideas spring from the study of various sociohistorical contexts of which they are part. Then one will also discover that, say, the American accentuation of "freedom" or "equality" involves highly ambiguous concepts whose meaning varies according to whether one's subject is the Constitution, the economy, minorities, or education. One would also realize that American culture is a contradictory affair in which ideas of self-restraint and ideas of high-level consumption are both affirmed, and in which self-reliance is proclaimed along with the idea of being dependent on commodities for one's personal happiness. In culture studies the student soon discovers that *context* is essential for the use and understanding of language – that the meaning of key cultural beliefs may vary according to the area or aspect of life to which they refer.

STEP 3 is then that of analyzing a text closely to see how these cultural assumptions are imbedded in the use of language itself. This, again, often involves an historical perspective. As the post-structuralists have argued, any text is an *intertext* at the same time. It often incorporates into itself idioms and formulas of prior texts, which require explanation before one can proceed to interpret the text in question. In Figure 6, the arrows reconnecting Step 3 with Steps 1 and 2 are meant to suggest that the textual analysis might be rounded off by resituating the text within the larger sociocultural discourse. As a text is only a particular expression of culture, it is natural in culture studies to conclude by redirecting the discussion to the larger cultural framework of which the text is only a part.

A Culture Studies Syllabus Exemplified

The syllabi of advanced and graduate courses in culture studies need little explanation. Whether the topic is "The Culture of Industrialism in 19th Century Britain" or "The Struggle for Civil Rights in the American South in the 1950s and 60s," the choice of subtopics and texts naturally reflects the particular interests of the individual teacher. Within the elementary, one-year study of English, however, the culture studies syllabus is intended to give university and college students a general introduction to American and British culture. In this connection it is also an open question whether culture studies should remain focused exclusively on these two cultures. The English language comprises a great many varieties spoken in various countries around the world with quite different cultures. There is no way, however, that these linguistic and cultural varieties can be taught within an already packed, one-year university program for beginner students of English as a foreign language.[6] For practical purposes, therefore, our teaching must remain largely limited to the British and American language and culture. None the less, even in such a one-year study of English a couple of literary works by for instance Indian, African, or Canadian writers may be included, along with brief introductions to the cultures in question. And at the graduate level one may certainly offer whatever course one wishes in English-speaking cultures other than the United Kingdom or the United States.

The number of cultural topics that could be taught within a basic course for beginner students of English is potentially unlimited, but certain general *subject areas* seem to have emerged at Scandinavian universities and colleges as appropriate constituents of a general, first year introduction to American culture. Although none of the areas of American life listed below may be regarded as absolutely imperative, together they may embody a useful introductory model:

<table>
<tr><td>*Regions*</td><td>*Foreign Policy*</td></tr>
<tr><td>*Immigration*</td><td>*Education*</td></tr>
<tr><td>*Economic System*</td><td>*Religion*</td></tr>
<tr><td>*Class Structure*</td><td>*Media/Popular Culture*</td></tr>
<tr><td>*Minorities*</td><td>*Arts/Material Culture*</td></tr>
<tr><td>*Gender/Women*</td><td>*Ideology*</td></tr>
<tr><td>*Government and Politics*</td><td></td></tr>
</table>

This framework leaves considerable leeway for choice and variation, depending on the interests of the teacher. Within each of these subject areas, a great many topics are possible, not all of which can be taught. Thus, an *exemplary* principle must be pursued. After a general introduction to each area of study, a particular topic may be chosen as an exemplary illustration. For example, after a brief characterization of the various regional cultures within the United States, the South may be chosen for in-depth study; after a brief introduction to minorities in the United States, one may proceed to concentrate on, say, the African Americans (or the Native Americans, or the Chicanos); within a presentation of the arts in America, one may choose to focus on the history of American painting; and so on within other subject areas. In the list of subjects above, the last item, ideology, functions as a summary of, and conclusion to, the entire course of American culture studies.

At the University of Tromsø these subject areas are packed into a one-semester intensive course; at the other Norwegian universitites a similar syllabus spans two semesters of teaching (with fewer hours each week). The introductory course in American culture at the University of Tromsø embodies two hours of lectures and two hours of seminar discussions each week (likewise with regard to British civilization). In American culture studies, the teaching of these subject areas follows the tripartite procedure of social, cultural, and textual analysis. The first lecture hour supplements and discusses the sociohistorical information given in the students' set textbooks on a particular subject of American life. The second lecture hour proceeds from this social perspective to a cultural one by focusing on the belief systems that serve to legitimize such sociohistorical matters – the assumptions which guide, say, the foreign policy of the United States. In the two-hour group discussions some of these cultural assumptions are pursued further, particularly in connection with close analysis of the language of very brief texts.

The choice of primary cultural texts for close analysis depends wholly on the individual teacher. Below are listed the American texts used at the University of Tromsø in connection with the teaching of "Gender" and the concluding session on "Ideology":

GENDER

A "Victorian" text (1835) extolling the virtues of the weaker sex
The Seneca Falls Declaration on Women's Rights (1848)
A passage from a hard-boiled detective novel
A passage from a woman's romance
An excerpt from a present-day feminist essay
Four advertisements directed at women
Three advertisements directed at men

The language in the passages from the popular novels is analyzed for its encoding of conventional sex roles, to be counterbalanced by the ideology of androgyny in the feminist text. The study of the women's advertisements serves to reveal different stereotypical ideas about femininity, and two of the male-oriented advertisements are studied for the way in which they combine the myth of the American West with traditional ideas of masculinity.

IDEOLOGY

The Declaration of Independence
Lincoln's "Gettysburg Address"
Question and answer from Ann Landers' Personal Advice Column
Excerpt from President Reagan's 1986 "State of the Union Address"
Excerpt from an interview with a corporate executive
Excerpt from Dale Carnegie, How to Win Friends and Influence People
Two passages from Arthur Miller, Death of a Salesman

The *Declaration of Independence* and the "Gettysburg Address" are here studied for their ideas of freedom and democracy; the particular Ann Landers' column for its philosophy of "God helps those who help themselves"; President Reagan's speech and the interview with the executive for dominant beliefs and values such as Manifest Destiny, individualism and competitiveness, progress and growth; and the Dale Carnegie and Arthur Miller excerpts for their 20th century version of success through appearance, personality, and being well liked.

With some exceptions, the texts used in the course on American culture are non-literary ones, but some of them are chosen for their expression of themes that are also found in works on the American literary syllabus – and vice versa. Thus, I would argue for a rough division of labor between the study of literature and culture studies, the former dealing with literary texts and the latter using mainly non-literary texts. This division of labor should by no means, however, be regarded as absolute; literary studies may make use of non-literary texts, and vice versa. The two disciplines make use of similar techniques of interpretation, but their objectives differ and require different approaches. Due to its concern with the representative and typical, the study of non-literary texts requires extensive sociohistorical knowledge. This knowledge is also necessary because non-literary texts tend to be quite closely bound up with an actual, sociocultural framework of a sender-message-receiver – in short with a particular socio-economic and cultural context. Non-literary texts therefore tend to illustrate the interplay between language and culture more directly than do literary texts, whose codes of fictionality make their relations to actual referents less specific and less situation-dependent. Understanding of the language of non-literary texts thus requires specific sociocultural insight, and, conversely, specific sociocultural insight requires the understanding of the language of particular historical texts.

The courses in American culture studies at the intermediate and graduate levels of the study of English at the University of Tromsø are of course more specialized and advanced, but the same tripartite analytical approach (from society through culture to text) is pursued here. Moreover, because this three-step methodology of culture studies has been firmly established in the one-year introductory study, the courses at the intermediate and graduate levels are more free to combine the fields of American civilization and literature. "Pure" American literature courses and "pure" culture courses are sometimes offered at the University of Tromsø, but more often interdisciplinarity is a main objective – the attempt to integrate these two fields of study. In such courses, non-literary texts are studied as closely as literary ones, and neither type of text serves merely as a "background" for the other. In this manner, students become even more aware, at the advanced levels of English, of the close interrelations and interconnections between the studies of culture and imaginative literature.

The Teaching of Two Topics Exemplified

In order to make the general syllabus and methodology of culture studies more concrete, let me link them to two limited, specific topics of

American culture studies, the first (within the subject of American government) the division of power between the federal government and the states, and the second (within the subject of gender) the ideology of femininity that one could call "The Feminine Mystique."[7] We may then illustrate the methodology of culture studies by the charts in Figure 7.

Figure 7. The Three-Step Analysis Applied to Two Particular Topics

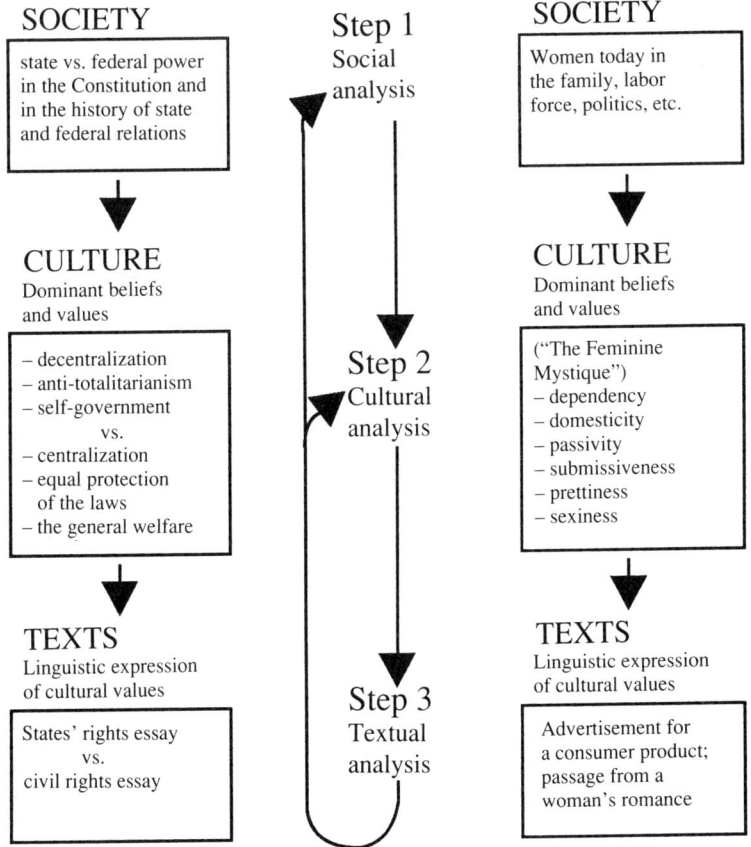

In these charts, the final summing-up – the cultural recapitulation – is indicated by the left-hand arrows in the middle column. The cultural assumptions specified in the figure are of course selective ones. Other patterns of beliefs and values could also have served as illustrations of these two subject areas of American culture.

As indicated by the left-hand column of the figure above, STEP 1 in the teaching of the topic of state vs. federal power in the United States may include a brief sketch of the historical development that led the country to become a *union* of *states*. One could also make the students examine the relevant passages in the Constitution that deal with this (not least the controversy surrounding the meaning of the l0th Amendment). Then one may move on to examine the history of federal and state relations, and end with a discussion of what sociopolitical areas the states today administer themselves, and what powers have been assumed by the federal Government itself.

STEP 2 of the analysis, however, may start with a discussion of the political considerations and assumptions that led the Founding Fathers to devise such a system of shared power, before one goes on to discuss various beliefs and values concerning state vs. federal power in the United States today. As to STEP 3, that of textual analysis, it would be illuminating to use a states' rights essay, for example the following from an article of l957 by James Jackson Kilpatrick:

> I hold this truth to be self-evident: That government is least evil when it is closest to the people. I submit that when effective control of government moves away from the people, it becomes a greater evil, a greater restraint upon liberty.
>
> My object is not to prove that the powers and functions of government have grown steadily more centralized, more remote from the people, for that proposition requires no proof; it requires only that one opens one's eyes. . . .
>
> -----
>
> I do not despair. So long as the I-beams and rafters of the Constitution remain undisturbed, the ravages of the Federal encroachment may be repaired. A latent yearning for personal liberty, an inherited resentment against the authoritarian state, a drowsing spirit of independence – these may yet be awakened. But, again, the States, as States, will have to do it.[8]

The language of this text is particularly interesting for its Jeffersonian echoes and its modern evocation of the ideas that led to the American Revolution and that are reflected for example in the Declaration of Independence. The text becomes particularly intriguing, however, when considered in the context in which it was published: in the wake of the commotion engendered in the South by the 1954 Supreme Court Decision of *Brown vs. Board of Education of Topeka,* which declared that segregated schools were unconstitutional because they deprived Blacks of the equal protection of the laws guaranteed by the l4th Amendment to the Constitution. An interpretation of this text must thus attempt to balance on the razor-sharp edge between, on the one hand, recognizing the importance and legitimacy, in various areas of American life, of many of the ideas formulated in this excerpt and, on the other hand, examining the sociocultural function that the formulation of these ideas is made to serve in this particular case concerning civil rights in the South.

The latter analysis may be facilitated by the use of an additional text that assumes the federal point of view, as does this excerpt from a newspaper article of 1963 by the historian Henry Steele Commager:

> The most notorious, and historically the most decisive, use of the doctrine of states' rights was, of course, to protect the institution of Negro slavery. States' rights were invoked, too, to delay expansion into the West, to defeat the regulation of trusts and railroads, to frustrate prohibition of child labor, to hold up the grant of suffrage to women, and to oppose social security, the conservation of natural resources, the creation of hydroelectric power for national purposes, the encouragement of public education and the protection of equality. . . .
>
> -----
>
> Certainly it would be asking a great deal to ask Negroes to believe that the national Government has been the enemy of freedom, and the states the guardians of freedom. It would be asking a great deal to ask labor to subscribe to the doctrine that it should look to the states, not to the nation, for the preservation of its rights.[9]

After analyzing the ideas evoked by Commager's language and specific references, one may recapitulate the conflicting ideologies involved and round off the discussion of state vs. federal power by looking at the situation in present-day America, particularly the positions assumed by the current Administration as well as by the Supreme Court with regard to states' rights and civil rights. In the latter instance, the issue of abortion provides a particularly incisive illustration of this controversy today.

At some point in the discussion, it would also be useful to compare the American federal-state-local distribution of powers to, for example, the Norwegian system, so as to make the students grasp the cultural differences involved. In our teaching of a foreign culture, a comparative perspective becomes important as a pedagogical means of motivation: the question of cultural similarities and dissimilarities is always an interesting one for non-native students. It is doubly educational as well: not only does it make students understand the nuances of the foreign culture better, it also makes them acquire a more conscious attitude to their own culture.

The same kind of three-step analysis may as easily be applied to the teaching of traditional assumptions about femininity in the United States, graphically presented by the right-hand column of Figure 7. STEP 1 may consist of a lecture on the situation of American women today in terms of family life, work, leisure, representation in business, participation in politics, and so on. STEP 2 may then involve the study of traditional beliefs and values concerning women. Here I have only focused on some of the most *stereotyped* culture patterns of the so-called "Feminine Mystique"; in my teaching of the subject of women these patterns are, as previously mentioned, counterbalanced by a discussion of *feminist* cultural ideas in the United States.

As to STEP 3, that of textual analysis, one could for instance use an example from an endless series of advertisements for Virginia Slims cigarettes, which has been running for years in American magazines and which is still going strong. The strategy is the same in many of these advertisements: one or more small, black-and-white photographs seemingly from the turn-of-the-century lives of women are contrasted to a large picture in color of a slim and smiling young woman, dressed for lesisure, accompanied by the subtitle: "You've come a long way, baby." In one advertisement, for example, a Victorian, cigar-smoking man has his dog bring him his newspaper and his wife bring him his slippers and is seen patting them both approvingly on the head. The caption ironically sums up the scene: "Back then, a woman always got equal pay for equal work"[10] – suggesting that a woman's life at that time was very much a dog's life. Our analysis of this caption should try to bring out its historical, feminist, and civil rights echoes. In the advertisement it is of course used ironically, but the impression evoked here of modern sex-role progressiveness should be counterbalanced by the observation that, in these advertisements, the present-day Virginia Slims woman is hardly ever depicted as working at all. She is usually presented in leisure-oriented and freewheeling terms; the image of a dog's carefree life may not be so far-fetched after all.

The interpretation of the Virginia Slims motto,"You've come a long way, baby," could in this connection serve to reveal how ambiguous this combination of having come "a long way" and "baby" is – what a fundamentally divided cultural vision this use of language gives expression to. This cultural split may already have been brought out by our STEP 2 discussion of the values of a feminine mystique vs. feminism. At the same time a comparative perspective may be useful. One may pose the question whether dominant Norwegian assumptions about women reflect a similar ambivalence. The issue may also be raised whether American society is particularly split because it was on the one hand marked by an exceptionally intense fight for women's rights in the 1960s and 70s, and on the other hand characterized by a strongly competitive ideology in which masculinist individual-centered and achievement-oriented values seek to relegate women to a passive and dependent role as nurturant beings, ornamental images of leisure, and/or sex objects.

This discussion of "the Feminine Mystique" could be supplemented by other texts with gender-marked language – for example an excerpt like the following from a woman's romance in which the hero and heroine embrace and kiss each other:

> As they stood bathing in this new found togetherness and each other's nearness, Heather turned soft blue eyes up to him and smiled slowly, her lips moist and parted. Brandon needed no other invitation to taste their honey sweetness. He lowered his head and his mouth moved over hers hungrily, and seeming by magic Heather turned in his arms and melted more closely to him, slipping her hands behind his back. His arm tightened about her waist and his other encircled her shoulders, crushing her to him, and she clung to him, wanting the moment to go on forever. His kiss filled her with desire, leaving every muscle in her body weak and pliable. She felt his thighs hard pressed against her own and realized his passion matched hers. Her lips parted under his mounting fervor and she rose on her toes to fit herself more intimately with his body.[11]

The imagery here evokes an extremely traditional vision of male-female relations. In addition to having "soft" eyes, lips of "sweetness," and muscles "weak and pliable," the woman "melted," "clung," and "fit herself" with the man's body. Admittedly there are some signs of activity on her part; her smile is an "invitation" with "moist and parted" lips, and her passion is described as equal to his, yet it is the man who is portrayed as active and she as merely reactive. He is the one who fills *her* with desire; with "tightened" arms and "thighs hard pressed," he is "crushing her to him," his "mounting fervor" causing her lips to part. Encoded in the descriptive language of this brief excerpt is thus an extended ideology of male dominance and female dependency and submissiveness.

At the end of the analyses of the Virginia Slims advertisement and the romance excerpt, one could, by way of a sociocultural recapitulation, discuss the representativeness of such texts for the lives and actual situation of women in the United States today. If such a sex-role study could serve to make many men (and some women) less masculinist in their thinking, the corresponding function of culture studies in general would be to make our students less ethnocentric. This does not, however, exclude the concept of a critical ethical perspective. The human suffering that particular ideologies help to produce and legitimize – for example in the case of race or religion – is sometimes formidable. This reverse side of the cultural-ideological coin also deserves attention in our teaching.

A generation ago, a guiding ideal (seldom attained) in foreign language teaching was that the student should become so well versed in English that he or she could be taken for a native English(wo)man (or American). This is an undesirable goal as well as a highly unrealistic one. In its non-literal sense, the phrase *to speak the same language* may mean *to agree,* but the aim of our study of dominant assumptions and values in America or Britain is not at all to make our students *think like* Americans or British people; it is only to make our students *understand* these people's ways of thinking as imbedded in their use of English. Understanding does not exclude criticism, quite the reverse. A comprehensive understanding of the discourse in which people's language is situated is the prerequisite for a genuine exchange of points of view, whether it is for business or pleasure, whether one negotiates a contract or speaks as a visitor – or, say, works as a foreign language teacher.

Notes

1 Elizabeth Fox-Genovese, "Between Individualism and Fragmentation: American Culture and the New Literary Studies of Race and Gender," *American Quarterly,* 42, No. 1 (March 1990), 9.
2 Fox-Genovese, "Between Individualism and Fragmentation," 23.
3 Sandemose, *Rejsen til Kjørkelvik* (København: Hans Reitzel, 1954), p. 104.
4 Noam Chomsky, "Syntax and Semantics," in J.P.B. Allen and Paul Van Buren, eds., *Chomsky: Selected Readings* (London: Oxford Univ. Press, 1971), p. 116.
5 Maidenform advertisement from *Cosmopolitan,* 196, no. 4 (April 1984), 173.
6 "Beginner university students of English": in Norway they have usually had nine years of English (on the average two-to-three hours a week) in elementary and secondary school prior to attending university.
7 The term, of course, is Betty Friedan's. See Friedan, *The Feminine Mystique* (New York: Norton, 1963).
8 Kilpatrick, "We the People as States," in Robert B. Dishman, ed., *The State of the Union: Commentaries on American Democracy* (New York: Scribner's, 1965), pp. 41, 50.
9 Commager, "To Form a Much Less Perfect Union," in Dishman, ed., *The State of the Union,* pp. 52, 53-54 (see note 8).
10 Virginia Slims advertisement from *Cosmopolitan,* 198, no. 4 (April 1985), 139.
11 Kathleen E. Woodiwiss, *The Flame and the Flower* (New York: Avon Books, 1972), p. 323.

9
The Scholarship of Textual Analysis: Culture Studies as a Research Discipline

The research characteristics of the discipline of culture studies cannot be considered in isolation from those of foreign language study in general. The subject of foreign-language study determines the nature of its culture studies research, and vice versa. Many humanist scholars, however, hold the view that foreign language studies is an institutional entity where the studies of linguistics, literature, and culture are brought together for teaching purposes only. Foreign language study is, as it were, simply a pedagogical matter. Its professors are, in terms of their research, either scholars of literature, linguistics, or culture, whose scientific projects are unconnected with the fact that they work within foreign language departments. A professor, say, of English literature is not considered a scholar whose field involves the interdisciplinary fusion of English and literature; he or she is regarded as a scholar of a literature that happens, so to speak, to be in English.

In my view, however, there are reasons other than mere didactic ones that make us insist to our students that a foreign language study represents an organic whole. It is not merely a subject taught, it represents a *study* – a comprehensive and systematic way of examining – a particular language, based on a combination of the subdisciplines of culture studies, linguistics, and literary studies. Interdisciplinarity should in fact be the central *research* objective of foreign language study – its ultimate scientific concern. Defined in this manner, foreign language study is, as suggested earlier, a field closely related to *philology,* which in the 1985 Humanities Report of the Norwegian Research Council is said to entertain "no natural divisions between the scholarly fields of history, linguistics, literature, and culture."[1]

In my opinion, foreign language study is essentially a philological field of study and its scholars philologists, regardless of the attempt in the above-mentioned Humanities Report to delimit the concept of philology by asserting that its methodological distinctiveness resides in its "reconstruction of [old] texts." The entry on philology in the Humanities Report concedes, however, that developments in the last decade or so may indicate that "the subject of philology could once again become a comprehensive cultural study, as it was in the last century."

But then the following sentence is ominously added in the Report (my italics): "Philology then becomes more of a *research program* than a *field of study* or a *science*."[2]

"Discipline" vs. "Area of Study": The Issue of "Scientificness"

The preoccupation in Scandinavia with the *Wissenschaftlichkeit* – the "scientificness" – of humanities disciplines is of course at odds with British and American usage, in which "science" is a term reserved for the natural, mathematical, and (oddly enough) social sciences, while "scholarship" is the appropriate humanist term. Such terminological differences notwithstanding, the field of culture studies faces the same dilemma within faculties in the United Kingdom and the United States as well as in Scandinavia; it meets opposition when trying to legitimize itself within the humanities as a scholarly field of research. The distinctions drawn above between "research program" and "field of study" deserve some discussion because they reflect a general confusion among academics as to what constitutes a "science" in the humanities. For example, by designating culture studies as a "didactic subject" rather than a "scientific field of study," the Humanities Report avoids including it among the academic "disciplines" proper.[3]

It would be unnecessary to devote any space to such terminological squabbles if it were not for the fact that they perform an important function in actual academic power struggles. The crux of the matter is that some subjects are traditional ones having won general recognition and acceptance, and some fields (like culture studies) are newcomers challenging the hegemony of these institutionalized compartmentalizations – not to mention the fact that they also turn into questions of academic positions and grants. As every student of language knows, the use of words also involves a process of naming, and naming is a source of power. Those who win acceptance for their names acquire considerable influence; those who do not have little leverage. It matters a lot, after all, whether one's subject is counted among the traditional disciplines and termed a "field of study" or whether one's subject is relegated to some baggy, supplementary entry and called an "area of study." If one's discipline, like that of culture studies, happens not to be part of those areas which today are given a certain priority (like to some extent Women's Studies or Media Studies), one becomes an "Other" that leads a meagre existence, both in terms of academic recognition and in terms of funds for research.

The rationale for these terminological distinctions seems to be that a "science," a "field of study," or a "discipline" has some sort of unified perspective and methodological distinctiveness, which an "area of study," "research program," or purely "didactic" subject lacks. Such a conception is nevertheless quite problematic. Some scholars would indeed argue that a scientific field is important and exciting as long as it reflects sharply differing views and approaches, and would welcome theoretical diversity rather than homogeneity, and methodological disagreement rather than unanimity. Both linguistics and literary study are cases in point; they make use of a great many, quite diverse models and methods acquired from neighboring subjects. The developments within the humanities over the last twenty years testify furthermore to the growing importance of such shared approaches as hermeneutics, structuralism, or semiotics, which are truly *trans*-disciplinary in the sense that each of them represents an overarching, interpretive approach to a great number of fields. Thus, ideas of methodological distinctiveness or a uniform approach cannot be used as criteria for accepting some university subjects as traditional academic "fields of study" and for dismissing others as merely "areas of study." Instead, it could be argued that the fields of the humanities can best be distinguished from each other in terms of their *subject matter* and the *type of material* they regard as their object of study.

There is, in short, no inherent reason to link the concept of "scientificness" to the term "field of study" rather than to an "area of study." "Scientificness" has to do with the systematic analysis of phenomena in order to establish theories about general principles and patterns that are seen to organize them; this is a matter of the character of specific research projects *within* a field or area of study, and should not be connected with academic fields as such or the way in which we classify them. At best, the term "scientific field of study" is mere tautology; at worst, it makes little sense and ought to be abolished, to the extent that it is abused so as to relegate certain academic subjects to a secondary role. Thus, there may be historical reasons, but hardly any theoretical, scientific ones, for regarding some humanities fields as scholarly disciplines and some as not – whether the subject in question is that of foreign language study in general or the discipline of culture studies in particular.

An Interdisciplinary Research Competence

It is not my intention in this chapter to give a general overview of the various approaches used in foreign language study in Scandinavia. Within the study of English there are a great many scholars who work with conventional linguistic, literary, and historical approaches, and a few who are either multidisciplinary or interdisciplinary in their orientation. My particular objective here is to present *one* specific interdisciplinary theory of the field of foreign language study and its culture studies component – one scientific, which is to say systematic and methodical, approach.

In this connection it is once again important to point out that the function of culture studies within the context of foreign language study is very different from that of cultural studies within a native context. As practised in the United Kingdom or the United States, British and American Studies may owe part of their academic distinction to their very inclusiveness, their attempt to embody a great many fields and areas of study. Although culture studies within the field of foreign language study may use the diverse findings of native cultural studies, its disciplinary range is per definition more narrow and involves particularly the interplay between culture and language.

As I see it, foreign language study may be defined in terms of its subject matter as the study of a particular foreign language as a means of communication. Within this field of study are three main scholarly disciplines: the studies of language, literature, and culture, respectively. Each of these three disciplines may also be defined in terms of its *subject matter* as the study of, respectively, the phonology and grammar of a particular language, its literary forms of expression, and its specific cultural discourses. Each of these studies also involves a particular type of *research material.* If the typical material for the formal analysis of language is conversational speech or the linguistic corpus, the main material for literary research is so-called fictional or "poetic" texts of the culture in which that language is spoken, and the predominant material for cultural research is the "non-literary" texts of that culture.

As previously argued, foreign language study and its three disciplinary components are in addition distinguished by their particular methodological focus, which is an interdisciplinary one. The concept of interdisciplinarity implies far more than mere dabbling in findings from different disciplines; it is intended to designate research based on a *fusion* of two or more disciplinary approaches – what Jay Mechling with yet another term has called *"convergent disciplinarity."*[4] The ultimate objective of a foreign language study is to demonstrate *scientifically* – in a systematic, scholarly manner – the interrelations between language, culture, and literature. Part of the aim of each of the disciplines of linguistic, cultural, and literary study is therefore to contribute to the explication and understanding of the two other components in this disciplinary triad.

Such research requires not only a *primary* competence in one's main discipline, but a *secondary* competence in the two others, which is exactly what a university education in, for example, English as a foreign language is intended to contribute to. As far as culture studies is concerned, however, there has been considerable dispute about the sort of qualifications required for a university position in this field. The description of positions in British and/or American civilization in the past has often involved formulations about a research competence in history or social science, with a possible proviso about additional documented work in some humanities field, for instance American or British philosophy, history of ideas, or art history. Requirements of this sort are in my opinion insufficient. Such a scholar's research will often remain within fields that have little connection with the nature of foreign language study, and she/he will probably fail to link her/his teaching to issues of linguistic or textual analysis.

The lack of consensus in Norway on the qualifications required for a position in culture studies has continued unabatedly to the present time. In connection with two recent civilization positions within the study of English, literature (or language) was given precedence in one case, and history in the other case. In my opinion both tendencies are detrimental to the development of culture studies as a discipline within the study of English as a foreign language. Instead, a position in culture studies should require interdisciplinary qualifications, more specifically a competence in the philological, text-oriented study of general cultural issues. This is something quite different from mere history, or linguistics, or literature taught in the English language.

As the attentive reader will have discovered, *culture studies* in this book has been consistently used in the singular in order to accentuate that it is a discipline, not some "area of study," some "program" taught by teachers who have their research qualifications in a different field and thus merely "teach" within this "subject area." If this were the case, then the prospects for developing the field would be bleak indeed. Each time new positions were filled, they would bring the field back to square one; appointed with qualifications in only, say, history or literature, the new scholars would have to train themselves, from the ground up, in the teaching of culture studies. At the same time, there would be no incentive for them to focus on research questions that would benefit the "program" in which they taught. Neither the subject of English nor the field of culture studies should rest satisfied with such a state of affairs.

The prevailing argument in each and every chapter of this book has instead been that culture studies is a discipline with its own subject matter, material of study, and research objectives. Embodying a particular theory of culture and a methodology combining social, cultural, and textual analysis, the field of culture studies requires specific interdisciplinary research qualifications brought to bear on the study of non-literary sources. Whether this analysis of texts is the result of a predominantly linguistic, literary, or historical orientation, it should be explicitly concerned with topics of a general cultural character, for example the dominant belief systems of a particular period, or the ideology of a particular movement, or the ideas and values of a particular social group. Only by requiring – for research fellowships as well as permanent positions – a general cultural competence combined with philological qualifications will culture studies develop as a discipline and refine its methods, its scope, and its insights.

Definition of Culture Studies as a Research Discipline

Systematic scholarship requires, however, a more precise definition of culture studies than this chapter has provided so far. As a point of departure we may use the general anthropological concept provided in Chapter 3, where culture is defined as dominant patterns of collective assumptions and values represented by the behavior of the members of a social group. The overriding objective of foreign language study will limit the concept of behavior mainly to *verbal behavior,* which in culture studies will be further limited mostly to *written* sources. Thus, for all practical purposes, *culture studies* may be defined as *the interpretation of a social group's dominant patterns of assumptions and values signified, explicitly or implicitly, by the language of non-literary texts.*

Such a *research* definition of the discipline as a text-oriented study takes the requisite historical, social, and political knowledge for granted. The emphasis on textual analysis is not meant to function as a straight-jacket; it is intended only as an indication of the core or nucleus of the discipline. Of course, other fields of study like the history of art, architecture, or music involve symbolic representations of behavior that can contribute significantly to cultural analysis; this is also true of the study of material culture. But the primary object of research within culture studies remains that of language as embodied in texts.

The concept of "text" must not, however, be regarded as something autonomous. It may be useful in this connection to keep in mind that any verbal act, any text, is, as Kenneth Burke puts it, *"symbolic action"* (with emphasis on both its semiotic and behavioral dimensions), *"a strategy for encompassing a situation,"* and thus "the *answer* or *rejoinder* to assertions current in the situation in which it arose."[5] In culture studies research, considerable attention is paid to the study of the sociocultural circumstances that produce a text, as well as to the analysis of the text as a reaction to this context. The only difference between culture studies as defined above and traditional philological studies is that, in the former instance, the conception of culture is more closely connected with everyday life and people's discourse in general. This does not exclude, however, possible analyses of more "élite," "high culture" texts as well. Texts to be used in culture studies should encompass everything from diaries, interviews, newspaper material, discursive prose, and documentary writing, through advertisements and comic strips, to political speeches, official documents, acts of Congress, and Supreme Court decisions.

When it comes to its basic approach, culture studies may start with the analysis of a variety of written sources of a certain period in order to be able to generalize about predominant patterns of ideas and values at that time, or it may start with a theory of these general culture patterns and see how they may or may not be embodied in the language of particular texts. Usually cultural research will consist of a combination of these inductive/deductive procedures. The concern with texts makes for a fusion of cultural and linguistic studies and makes manifest the cultural characteristics of linguistic communication as well as the linguistic characteristics of cultural communication. In addition, the close examination of the language of non-literary sources inevitably reveals that its means of expression are no different in kind from many of those used in literary works. Thus, culture studies research may contribute to the understanding of literary language and vice versa. In addition it may furnish an approach that may also be applied to the analysis of the cultural context that a literary work gives expression to. This is one illustration of how a systematic interdisciplinarity may be practised.

The relationship between foreign language study and its three disciplinary constituents represents a sort of hermeneutic circle; the whole (of foreign language study) defines the scholarly character of its parts (of linguistic, literary, and cultural studies), and the parts define the scholarly character of the whole. Consequently foreign language study is not so much a study of discrete phenomena as a study of *relationships,* and to analyze the relations between phenomena is different from analyzing their intrinsic characteristics. Thus, the objective of culture studies research within the field of foreign language study is *cognitively* different from the kind of cultural research carried out in other fields. To reduce it to some discipline like history or sociology is like sawing off a round table in order to get it through a doorway.

Culture Studies Research Exemplified

Let me illustrate these ideas of interdisciplinary study by referring to one of my own research projects, which involves the study of the interrelationships between American culture and imaginative literature in the 1920s. This study is particularly concerned with the strong ideological conflicts and contradictions in that decade between the traditional values inherited from an industrial production society (with its emphasis on hard work, self-denial, and character) and the increasingly pervasive assumptions of the mass consumption society emerging at this time (with its emphasis on leisure, self-gratification, and personality).

The analysis of the clashes between these belief systems requires first of all extensive historical research on this period. This involves the close study of a variety of non-literary texts. Such research is in turn necessary for the *cultural* interpretation of key literary works of this decade, particularly of the way in which their reaction to the culture of the 1920s can be said to be signified by their literary techniques and structures.

In the process of this research I also became interested in the advertising from this period, because it, formally speaking, seemed to me to develop from being *representational* at the beginning of the 1920s to being more *non-representational* towards the end of the decade – which is to say that advertisements turned from describing the inherent characteristics of the products to presenting them in terms of *something else*. The examination of this possible development from function-oriented to metaphorical techniques in advertising required the kind of quantitative, statistical analysis that typifies historical research. Thus, I went through the advertisements in different magazines from the years 1921, 1924-25, and 1929. But this work could not be kept separate from a qualitative perspective, as the question of predominantly representational or non-representational means of expression is inevitably a matter of interpretation.

The turning from a descriptive towards a metaphorical technique in advertising seemed to me to be closely connected with the historical transition from production-oriented to more consumption oriented values. Such a sociohistorical thesis then led me to wonder whether this trend within advertising served to characterize other types of texts as well – whether there was also for example a marked tendency in the newspaper language of the period to become less informational and more image-oriented. This in turn led me to speculate whether there could be any possible historical-cultural connection between such a general sociolinguistic development and the increasing use of *modernist* means of expression in the American literature of the 1920s – the growing dominance of an imagist and metaphorical style. In this manner, my research on the 1920s represented a constant interplay between cultural, linguistic, and literary perspectives.

Let me in conclusion examine the language of an advertisement from 1924 as an illustration of the interdisciplinarity that the field of culture studies in my opinion demands. This is an advertisement for the Jordan automobile, more precisely a model named *Playboy,* which featured the illustration of a young woman standing beside a horse on a hillside with a car below her, supplemented with the following text:

A Golden Girl from Somewhere

> When the Spring is on the mountain and the day is at the door – a golden girl from somewhere stands wondering, expectant, on the world's far edge.
>
> Somewhere beyond that unfathomable sky – beyond the purple hills – lie laughter and joy and smooth delight.
>
> Lithe and splendid, touched with a happy craving that will not be denied, she is going to the place where fairy tales come true.
>
> May she choose the Playboy for her companion to the end of the traveled road – then a wonderful horse on up the slope with Spring to the desolate lone of outer space.[6]

This advertisement represents an attempt to sell the automobile not in terms of a representational technique, not in terms of the inherent qualities and functions of the car, but in terms of an image that connects it with a vague but suggestive longing for a happiness that awaits somewhere in the blue distance. The only trace of a functional description is the implication that one uses the car to get to where the woman presently stands. Otherwise the function of the advertisement is purely metaphorical. The car is sold in terms of the leisure-and-entertainment ethos reflected in the longing for "laughter and joy and smooth delight," as well as in "a happy craving that will not be denied," a philosophy of instant gratification which may be seen as a direct counterpart to the earlier production-oriented emphasis on self-discipline and self-denial on the road towards future success.

This desire for gratification is expressed in extremely vague terms. The girl comes from "Somewhere" and is expectantly on her way to "Somewhere beyond," a place "where fairy tales come true." Research in historical sources like advertisers' trade journals and books reveals that such vague and dream-like language was meant to appeal particularly to women readers. At this time a surprisingly large number of automobile advertisements were directed specifically at women – certainly a larger part of the total car advertisements than is the case today. Women were themselves at times considered as potential buyers (Jordan's *Playboy* was a sports car rather than a family automobile), but even more important, perhaps, was the assumption in the advertising business that women often had considerable influence when it came to the family's choice of automobile. In this connection, advertisers often argued that the language that was to appeal to the female consumer should be "feminine," that is, assume a highly personal and suggestive tone. The editor of *The Woman's Home Companion* even suggested that "If I were trying to induce a woman to buy a fine automobile, for instance, I would picture to her a car that is the acme of luxury and loveliness; I would try to take her out of her mundane world and transport her into fairyland."⁷ The text of this advertisement consequently embodies something that was held in the 1920s to represent a typical, sales-oriented "woman's language." (This does not, of course, exclude the possibility of this advertisement appealing to the male consumer as well, particularly by way of its coupling together of the woman and the car.)

In addition to inviting such direct historical-linguistic observations, the advertisement also lends itself to a literary-oriented analysis by way of its use of imagery and symbols. The expression "golden girl" evokes connotations of luxury and wealth, of carefreeness and happiness, as well as associations of popularity and, most of all, romance (cf. "fairy tales come true"). Linked metaphorically with the girl, the car assumes a meaning that goes far beyond its significance as a means of transportation. At the end, the car and the horse seem to acquire parallel functions in terms of both syntax and semantics. Both the *Playboy* and the horse assume sexual overtones as their rider is carried to a sort of cosmic climax in "the desolate lone of outer space." The car is indeed sold in terms of attributes quite different from its inherently utilitarian ones.

Some of the grammatical features of the text also deserve comment. The expression "May she choose the Playboy" is for example interesting; it is no direct appeal or exhortation, but instead a formulaic phrase expressing hope and wish, often on others' behalf (as in "May you live long and be happy"). Thus, the appeal about purchasing the *Playboy* almost assumes the character of a blessing. The linguistic vagueness previously mentioned is also accentuated in grammatical terms by way of the use of the indefinite article: "*a* golden girl," "*a* happy craving," and "*a* wonderful horse," along with the fronting of the word "somewhere" in the sentence "Somewhere beyond . . . lie laughter," giving the adverb thematic prominence. But far more interesting in this connection is perhaps the use of the *definite* form of the noun where one could just as appropriately expect the noun to be preceded by *zero* or *indefinite* article: "*the* Spring is on the mountain," "Somewhere beyond *that* unfathomable sky – beyond *the* purple hills," "*the* place where fairy tales come true." Grammatically speaking such a technique makes this dreamy mishmash assume an *apparently* definite form; the extremely vague place descriptions seem more concrete, as if they actually did exist somewhere. The woman reader is thus introduced to a hazy landscape of longings whose indeterminateness (and fictive status) is at the same time glossed over and obscured. In this manner purely grammatical constructions can be said to assume a particular cultural function.

Most striking in this advertisement is perhaps the final, non-finite sentence "then a wonderful horse on up the slope . . ." As a linguist colleague of mine exclaimed when we discussed the grammar of this text: "Where is the *verb?* What does she do with that horse?" This syntactic observation brings us back to the sexual motif of the literary-oriented analysis, which arose from the connotations around the playboy-and-horse symbolism.

The interpretation of the text of this advertisement has consequently proceeded from historical research on the American 1920s (in particular its dominant consumption-oriented assumptions and its view of women's language), through an analysis of the advertisement's metaphorical technique and its literary-oriented means of expression, to a linguistic discussion of some of its grammatical and syntactic features, which in turn throws light upon the cultural-thematic implications of the advertisement. Research within foreign language study ought to be characterized by precisely a synthesis of linguistics, literary analysis, and culture studies. Culture, it repeatedly turns out, is language, and language is culture, and mixed into it all – more often than one would think – are a great many so-called "literary" techniques.

Notes

1 Rådet for humanistisk forsking [the Humanities Research Board], Norges almenvitenskapelige forskningsråd [the Norwegian Research Council for Science and the Humanities], *Humanistisk forsking i Noreg: Eigenart, målsetjing og utviklingstendensar (Humaniorautgreiinga,* del II) *[Humanist Research in Norway: Characteristics, Objectives, and Future Trends (The Humanities Report, Part II)]* (Oslo, 1985), p. 12.
2 The Humanities Report, Part III, pp. 36-37, 38.
3 The Humanities Report, Part III, p. 12.
4 Mechling, "Languaging American Studies," *The American Examiner*, 2, no. 2 (Winter 1974), 6.
5 Burke, *The Philosophy of Literary Form* (Berkeley: Univ. of California Press, 1973), pp. 8, 109.
6 Jordan car advertisement from *Saturday Evening Post,* 196 (March 29, 1924), 84.
7 Gertrude Lane quoted in Carl A. Naether, *Advertising to Women* (New York: Prentice-Hall, 1928), p. 27.

10
Overarching Synthesis: The Study of English as a whole

The preceding chapters on the didactics and scholarship of the discipline of culture studies have sought to present a comprehensive interdisciplinary theory of its cognitive objectives within the study of English as a foreign language. As far as the study of English as a whole is concerned, however, it is not enough to have culture studies become interdisciplinary if the two other disciplines of linguistics and literary study remain unconnected with culture studies and with each other. Although most syllabus descriptions of the study of English include observations on the importance of the integration of these three disciplines, present-day practice in the teaching of English falls short even of these modest aims. Of course students have to be provided with the basic disciplinary tools and methods before teaching can proceed to interdisciplinary perspectives, but this latter step is rarely implemented. Students repeatedly complain that the disciplines of linguistics, literary study, and culture studies seem to have little connection with each other, and that teachers rarely make references to the other disciplines in their classes. The linguist, the professor of literature, and the scholar of culture studies have the hallmarks of three characters who are less than half-heartedly in search of an author.

Some Modest Didactic Proposals

In this connection I have some practical, didactic recommendations for making the study of English somewhat more integrated than at present. First of all, I would like to suggest that scholars within the three disciplines make more use of each other's teaching materials. It does not require very much work for, say, teachers of linguistics to select some of their analytical material from the texts of the literary and cultural syllabuses. Nor does it require very much effort for the culture studies and literature teachers to refer to each other's texts and to make use of some linguistics material in order to analyze it from a cultural or literary point of view. Indeed, teachers in the three disciplines should collaborate on the selection of textual and conversational samples that would be usable for all parties involved. Finding the same material used in different classes, the students would discover that the various disciplinary approaches represent different means to the same end — the acquisition and analysis of language. These more or less token gestures would help make the study of English appear less fragmented than is the case at present.

But we may also take this one step further. Most of the scholars in the English department should at least take the trouble to acquaint themselves with the few introductory books that are required reading in the three disciplines for beginner university students of English. This would make teachers acquire a tri-disciplinary vocabulary that they could introduce in the teaching of their own subject. Thus, for instance, literature and culture studies teachers could, in their textual analysis, use grammatical terms like "mass/count nouns," "finite/non-finite sentences," "coordinate/subordinate clauses," and so on, thus making the students aware that what they learn in linguistics is relevant for the understanding of literary and cultural texts as well. And the linguists could more often make use of terms like "imagery," "figure of speech" ("simile," "metaphor," "symbol"), "narrative," "dominant beliefs," "cultural values," and so on, which would cause the students to realize that literary and cultural interpretations are not something which exist apart from linguistic analysis. In this manner, the majority of the teachers would contribute to the impression that the subject of English involves a shared terminology and represents some sort of unity.

Such pragmatic efforts would certainly constitute a pedagogical improvement on the state of affairs at present, but they would not necessarily represent much of an advance in terms of scholarship — and continuous research is the prerequisite for the existence and development of any study at the university level. Paying what could become mere lip-service to the idea of integration is, in the long run, to do English a disservice as an academic study. The modest didactic recommendations above must therefore be supplemented by a scholarly, research-oriented pursuit of the idea of interdisciplinarity.

The Need for a Research Commitment to Interdisciplinarity

To become familiar with, and try to integrate, theories, methods, and practices within several disciplines is a demanding intellectual activity, but the foundation necessary to begin such work is after all already laid in foreign language studies. From the elementary level to graduate studies, the students of for example English are introduced to courses in both language and literature as well as culture studies. Most other academic subjects are far more uniform and homogeneous in comparison. The competence provided by a study such as English is distinctive because of its multiple disciplinary perspectives, which should offer the best possible point of departure for interdisciplinary work.

Yet many attitudes within academia actually seem to disparage such a specifically philological competence. As mentioned in the previous chapter, there are professors of, for example, English language or literature who regard themselves primarily as scholars of linguistics or literary studies whose teaching merely takes place, as it were, in an English department. In debates at the department or faculty level, scholars all too often seem more motivated by protecting their narrow disciplinary interests than by promoting the study of English as a whole. And, to take another example, in the guidelines and reports of the Norwegian Humanities Research Council there has been no separate entry so far for the philologically oriented scholarship that typifies foreign language studies; such scholarship has traditionally been classified as either belonging to linguistics or to literary studies. There is even a tendency among philological scholars themselves to regard research of a theoretical or generic nature as somehow more prestigious than scholarship that involves the close intrinsic or contextual analysis of a particular corpus or text.

In all these cases, the idea of philology is overlooked or depreciated. This is not to say that philologists cannot pursue strictly literary or linguistic subjects. Diversity of research interests among academics is a prerequisite for a dynamic scholarly milieu, and new insights within disciplines may help produce new insights between them, and vice versa. Of course, scholars in foreign language departments may also commit themselves to strictly theoretical research projects within linguistics or literature, just as scholars within departments of general/comparative literature or general linguistics may choose to do research on particular texts. It is equally obvious, however, that scholars of for instance comparative literature develop a particular competence in theoretical and genre-oriented studies, whereas literary scholars of philology acquire special qualifications in a national literature, more specifically in the analysis of the particular linguistic-cultural texture of literary works.

What consequently makes a foreign language subject such as English distinctive is precisely its combined linguistic, literary, and cultural perspectives. If the integration of these disciplines is to progress further within the teaching of English, however, more scholars must commit themselves to interdisciplinary research. Such integration would also make headway if new or vacant positions and research fellowships were to be advertised with an emphasis on the desirability of an interdisciplinary orientation.

We all have our ideal visions that help nourish our engagement in the nitty-gritty of everyday institutional life, and this is one of mine: I am being invited to build an English department from the bottom up — funding being no obstacle, of course. In no time I have peopled my department with scholars whose work within their own field is extensive and exceptional, but who have also done considerable interdisciplinary research, particularly into the interconnections between language, culture, and literature. Thus, in their teaching, they introduce the students to the main tools and major modes of thinking within their particular discipline, but they also proceed, once this basic foundation is laid, to make the students aware of how linguistic discourse can only be fully comprehended from a general philological perspective. As my scholars are all to a considerable degree acquainted with the work carried out in the other two fields, they mutually inspire and criticize each others' scholarship. In their exchanges on research, the linguists become excited by their colleagues' insight into the cultural and creative dimensions of language, the culture scholars' theses are constantly enriched by the others' literary and syntactic-grammatical approaches, and the professors of literature find their texts assuming linguistic and cultural dimensions that vastly expand their interpretive possibilities.

As research in these disciplines becomes enriched and their boundaries expanded, new insights are engendered for the study of English as a whole. The milieu of the students is in turn affected by this collaboration between the teachers. They too begin to see that the study of language cannot be compartmentalized, and that the foreign language that they are learning to analyze from an integrated humanities perspective is a systematic and suggestive, referential and figurative, rule-governed and variegated, means of communication.

Of course this vision is pure wish fulfillment for financial as well as other reasons. New positions in the humanities today are few and far between, and the spirit of collectivism evoked above runs counter to the deep-rooted individualistic character of most scholarship within the humanities. None the less, however short we may fall of ideal aims, we must not cease to give integration a high priority.

In this book, the field of culture studies has been conceived as a philological, textual study of culture, or, with a slight reversion of emphasis, as a philological, cultural study of texts. The discipline of culture studies consequently requires the fusion of analytical methods from the fields of anthropology, linguistics, history, and literary studies. Not merely the sum of different fields but the study of the relations between them, culture studies is not merely multidisciplinary but interdisciplinary.

A similar integrative orientation is also needed in linguistic and literary studies within the study of English as a foreign language. There are numerous areas of enquiry within English about which we need to know more, and in which there is consequently an urgent need for interdisciplinary research, be it into the interrelations between language use and ideology, between everyday speech and literary language, or between hegemonic culture patterns and the structures of imaginative literature. If foreign-language study is to develop as an academic field, it is to such and similar philological enquiries that long-term research must be devoted. Interdisciplinarity is not merely a pedagogical issue; it is the scholarly prerequisite for increasing our understanding of the study of English as a whole. And, as far as the discipline of culture studies is concerned, it is my hope that this book has helped clear the theoretical and methodological ground necessary for such a philological understanding.

Bibliography: Works cited

Allen, J.P.B. and Paul Van Buren, eds. *Chomsky: Selected Readings*. London: Oxford University Press, 1971.
Atkinson, Brooks, ed. *The Selected Writings of Ralph Waldo Emerson*. New York: Modern Library, 1950.
Austin, J.L. *How to Do Things with Words*. Cambridge, Mass.: Harvard University Press, 1962.
Bakhtin, M.M. *The Dialogic Imagination*. Austin: Univ. of Texas Press, 1981.
Bateson, Gregory. *Mind and Nature: A Necessary Unity*. New York: Bantam Books, 1979.
Bateson, Gregory. *Steps to an Ecology of Mind*. New York: Ballantine Books, 1972.
Becker, Carl. "Everyman His Own Historian." *American Historical Review*, 37, no. 2 (January 1932), 221-236.
Becker, Carl. "What Are Historical Facts?" *Western Political Quarterly*, 8, no. 3 (September 1955), 327-340.
Berkhofer, Robert. *A Behavioral Approach to Historical Analysis*. New York: Free Press, 1969.
Berkhofer, Robert. "Clio and the Culture Concept: Some Impressions of a Changing Relationship in American Historiography." *Social Science Quarterly*, 53 (1972), 297-320.
Bock, Philip. *Modern Cultural Anthropology: An Introduction*. New York: Knopf, 1969.
Bowron, Bernard, Leo Marx, and Arnold Rose. "Literature and Covert Culture." In Joseph J. Kwiat and Mary C. Turpie, eds. *Studies in American Culture: Dominant Ideas and Images*. Minneapolis: University of Minnesota Press, 1960, pp. 84-95.
Bradbury, Malcolm and David Palmer, eds. *Contemporary Criticism*. London: Edward Arnold, 1970.
Fredrik Chr. Brøgger. "A Cultural Approach to American Studies," *American Studies in Scandinavia*,12 (1980), 1-15.
Fredrik Chr. Brøgger. "For å kommunisere må man forstå andres tenkesett: Kulturkunnskapen i engelskundervisningen i den videregående skolen." *Språk og språkundervisning*, 12, no. 4 (1979), 39-44.
Fredrik Chr. Brøgger. "Grinding the Gears of Production and Consumption: Representational versus Nonrepresentational Advertising for Automobiles in the Mid-1920s." *Prospects*, 15 (1990), 197-224.
Burke, Kenneth. *Language as Symbolic Action*. Berkeley: Univ. of California Press, 1966.
Burke, Kenneth. *The Philosophy of Literary Form*. Berkeley: University of California Press, 1973.
Børtnes, Jostein. "Filologi og studiet av fremmedspråkenes kultur." In *Kulturkunnskap som forskningsfag*. Oslo: Rådet for humanistisk forskning, NAVF, 1988, pp. 46-56.
Cady, Edwin H. "'American Studies' in the Doldrums: Or Whistling Up a Breeze." In Robert Merideth, ed. *American Studies: Essays on Theory and Method*. Columbus, Ohio: Charles E. Merrill, 1968, pp. 33-39.
Caughey, John L. "Ethnography, Introspection, and Reflexive Culture Studies." *Prospects*, 7 (1982), 115-139.

Chomsky, Noam. *Syntactic Structures*. The Hague: Mouton, 1957.
Chomsky, Noam. "Syntax and Semantics." In J.P. B. Allen and Paul Van Buren, eds. *Chomsky: Selected Readings*. London: Oxford Univ. Press, 1971, pp. 101-126.
Cole, Peter and Jerry L. Morgan, eds. *Syntax and Semantics*, vol. III: *Speech Acts*. New York: Academic Press, 1975.
Commager, Henry Steele. "To Form a Much Less Perfect Union." In Robert B. Dishman, ed. *The State of the Union: Commentaries on American Democracy*. New York: Scribner's, 1965, pp. 51-56.
de Saussure, Ferdinand. *Course in General Linguistics*. New York: Philosophical Library, 1959.
Despard, Annabelle. "On the Teaching of British Civilisation." *Språk og språkundervisning*, 17, no. 1 (1984), 47-58.
Despard, Annabelle. "Multi-Cultural Education – A Special Need for All." In John Oakland, ed. "Working Papers in Civilisation Topics and Research," Vol. 2. Trondheim, Norway: University of Trondheim, English Institute, 1985, pp. 49-72.
Dishman, Robert B. *The State of the Union: Commentaries on American Democracy*. New York: Scribner's, 1965.
DuBois, Cora. "The Dominant Value Profile of American Culture." *American Anthropologist*, 57 (1955), 1232-1239.
Emerson, Ralph Waldo. "Self-Reliance." *The Selected Writings of Ralph Waldo Emerson*, ed. Brooks Atkinson. New York: Modern Library, 1950, pp. 145-169.
Empson, William. *Seven Types of Ambiguity*. Harmondsworth: Penguin, 1961.
Fernandez, James W. "Persuasions and Performances: Of the Beast in Every Body ... And the Metaphors of Everyman." In Clifford Geertz, ed. *Myth, Symbol, and Culture*. New York: Norton, 1971, pp. 39-60.
Feuer, Lewis S., ed. *Marx and Engels, Basic Writings on Politics and Philosophy*. London: Fontana, 1969.
Fish, Stanley. *Is There a Text in This Class?* Cambridge, Mass.: Harvard University Press, 1980.
Fishwick, Marshall W., ed. *American Studies in Transition*. Boston: Houghton Mifflin, 1969. First published by University of Pennsylvania Press, 1964.
Fitzgerald, F. Scott. *The Great Gatsby*. New York: Scribner's, 1925.
Fluck, Winfried. "Aesthetic Premises in American Studies." In Robin W. Winks, ed. *Other Voices, Other Views; An International Collection of Essays from the Bicentennial*. Westport, Conn.: Greenwood Press, 1978), pp. 21-30.
Fowler, Roger. "The Structure of Criticism and the Languages of Poetry: An Approach through Language." In Malcolm Bradbury and David Palmer, eds. *Contemporary Criticism*. London: Edward Arnold, 1970, pp. 172-194.
Fowler, Roger, and Gunther Kress. "Rules and Regulations" and "Critical Linguistics." In Roger Fowler, Bob Hodge, Gunther Kress, og Tony Trew. *Language and Control*. London: Routledge and Kegan Paul, 1979, pp. 26-45 and 185-213.
Fowler, Roger, Bob Hodge, Gunther Kress, and Tony Trew. *Language and Control*. London: Routledge and Kegan Paul, 1979.
Fox-Genovese, Elizabeth. "Between Individualism and Fragmentation: American Culture and the New Literary Studies of Race and Gender." *American Quarterly*, 42, No. 1 (March 1990), 7-34.
Friedan, Betty. *The Feminine Mystique*. New York: Norton, 1963.
Geertz, Clifford. "Ideology as a Cultural System." *The Interpretation of Cultures*. New York: Basic Books, 1973, pp. 193-233.
Geertz, Clifford. "The Impact of the Concept of Culture on the Concept of Man." *The Interpretation of Cultures*. New York: Basic Books, 1973, pp. 33-54.
Geertz, Clifford. *The Interpretation of Cultures*. New York: Basic Books, 1973.
Geertz, Clifford, ed. *Myth, Symbol, and Culture*. New York: Norton, 1971.
Geertz, Clifford. "Ritual and Social Change: A Javanese Example." *The Interpretation of Cultures*. New York: Basic Books, 1973, pp. 142-169.
Geertz, Clifford. "Thick Description: Toward an Interpretive Theory of Culture." *The Interpretation of Cultures*. New York: Basic Books, 1973, pp. 3-30.

Greimas, A.-J. *Structural Semantics: An Attempt at a Method.* Lincoln: University of Nebraska Press, 1983.
Grice, Paul H. "Logic and Conversation." In Peter Cole and Jerry L. Morgan, eds. *Syntax and Semantics,* vol. III: *Speech Acts.* New York: Academic Press, 1975, pp. 41-58.
Gulliksen, Øyvind. "Kulturkunnskapens plass i engelskfaget." *Språk og språkundervisning,* 11, no 4 (1978), 56-69.
Gunn, Giles. "American Studies as Cultural Criticism," *The Culture of Criticism and the Criticism of Culture.* New York: Oxford University Press, 1987, pp. 147-172.
Halliday, M.A.K. *Explorations in the Functions of Language.* London: Edward Arnold, 1973.
Halliday, M.A.K. *Language as Social Semiotic: The Social Interpretation of Language and Meaning.* London: Edward Arnold, 1978.
Henry, Jules. "A Theory for an Anthropological Analysis of American Culture." In Joseph G. Jorgensen and Marcello Truzzi, eds. *Anthropology and American Life.* Englewood Cliffs, N.J.: Prentice-Hall, 1974, pp. 6-22.
Higham, John. "American Intellectual History: A Critical Appraisal." In Robert Merideth, ed. *American Studies: Essays on Theory and Method.* Columbus, Ohio: Charlies E. Merrill, 1968, pp. 218-235.
Higham, John. "Hanging Together: Divergent Unities in American History." *Journal of American History,* 61 (June 1974), 5-28.
Higham, John, and Paul K. Conkin, eds. *New Directions in American Intellectual History.* Baltimore: Johns Hopkins University Press, 1979.
Humaniorautgreiinga, del II: Humanistisk forsking i Noreg. [The Humanities Report, Part II: Humanist Research in Norway]. Oslo: Rådet for humanistisk forsking [The Humanities Research Council], NAVF, 1985.
Inkeles, Alex and Daniel J. Levinson. "National Character: The Study of Modal Personality and Sociocultural Systems." In Gardner Lindzey and Elliot Aronson, eds. *The Handbook of Social Psychology,* Vol. IV. Reading, Mass.: Addison-Wesley, 1969, pp. 418-506.
Jaeger, Gertrude and Philip Selznick. "A Normative Theory of Culture." In Robert Merideth, ed. *American Studies: Essays on Theory and Method.* Columbus, Ohio: Charles E. Merrill, 1968, pp. 93-123.
Johnson, Richard. "The Story So Far: And Further Transformations?" In David Punter, ed. *Introduction to Contemporary Cultural Studies.* London: Longman, 1986, pp. 277-313.
Jorgensen, Joseph G. and Marcello Truzzi, eds. *Anthropology and American Life.* Englewood Cliffs, N.J.: Prentice-Hall, 1974.
Kilpatrick, James Jackson. "We the People as States." In Robert B. Dishman, ed. *The State of the Union: Commentaries on American Democracy.* New York: Scribner's, 1965, pp. 41-50.
Kluckhohn, Clyde and William H. Kelly. "The Concept of Culture." In Ralph Linton, ed. *The Science of Man in the World Crisis.* New York: Columbia University Press, 1945, pp. 78-106.
Kress, Gunther and Robert Hodge. *Language as Ideology.* London: Routledge and Kegan Paul, 1979.
Kreuger, Thomas A. "The Historians and the Edenic Myth: A Critique." *Canadian Review of American Studies,* 4, no. 1 (Spring 1973), 3-18.
Kroeber, A.L. and Clyde Kluckhohn. *Culture: A Critical Review of Concepts and Definitions.* New York: Vintage Books, 1963.
Kroeber, A.L., and Talcott Parsons. "The Concepts of Culture and of Social System." *American Sociological Review,* 23, no. 5 (1958), 582-583.
Kuhn, Thomas S. *The Structure of Scientific Revolutions,* Second Edition. Chicago: University of Chicago Press, 1970.
Kuklick, Bruce. "Myth and Symbol in American Studies." *American Quarterly,* 24 (October 1972), 435-450.
Kwiat, Joseph J. and Mary C. Turpie, eds. *Studies in American Culture: Dominant Ideas and Images.* Minneapolis: University of Minnesota Press, 1960.

Labov, William. *Language in the Inner City: Studies in the Black English Vernacular.* Oxford: Blackwell, 1972.
Labov, William. *Sociolinguistic Patterns.* Philadelphia: University of Pennsylvania Press, 1972.
Langer, Susanne K. *Philosophy in a New Key.* Cambridge, Mass.: Harvard University Press, 1957, first published 1942..
Leech, Geoffrey N. *Principles of Pragmatics.* London: Longman, 1983.
Lenz, Guenter H. "American Studies – Beyond the Crisis?: Recent Redefinitions and the Meaning of Theory, History, and Practical Criticism." *Prospects,* 7 (1982), 53-113.
Lewis, R.W.B. *The American Adam.* Chicago: University of Chicago Press, 1955.
Lindzey, Gardner and Elliot Aronson, eds. *The Handbook of Social Psychology,* Vol. IV. Reading, Mass.: Addison-Wesley, 1969.
Linton, Ralph, ed. *The Science of Man in the World Crisis.* New York: Columbia University Press, 1945.
Luedtke, Luther. "Not So Common Ground: Controversies in Contemporary American Studies." *The Study of American Culture: Contemporary Conflicts.* DeLand, Florida.: Everett/ Edwards, 1977, pp. 323-367.
McDowell, Tremaine. *American Studies.* Minneapolis: University of Minnesota Press, 1948.
Malamud, Bernard. *Dubin's Lives.* New York: Avon Books, 1979.
Marx, Karl. "Preface to *A Contribution to the Critique of Political Economy.*" In Lewis S. Feuer, ed. *Marx and Engels, Basic Writings on Politics and Philosophy.* London: Fontana, 1969, pp. 83-87.
Marx, Leo. *The Machine in the Garden.* New York: Oxford University Press, 1964.
Marx, Leo. "American Studies – A Defense of an Unscientific Method." *New Literary History,* 1 (1969), 77-90.
Mechling, Jay. "If They Can Build a Square Tomato: Notes Toward a Holistic Approach to Regional Studies." *Prospects,* 4 (1979), 59-77.
Mechling, Jay. "Languaging American Studies," *The American Examiner,* 2, No. 2 (1974), 6.
Mechling, Jay, Robert Merideth, and David Wilson. "American Culture Studies: The Discipline and the Curriculum." *American Quarterly,* 25 (October 1973), 363-389.
Merideth, Robert, ed. *American Studies: Essays on Theory and Method.* Columbus, Ohio: Charles E. Merrill, 1968.
Merideth, Robert, "Introduction: Theory, Method and American Studies." *American Studies: Essays on Theory and Method.* Columbus, Ohio: Charles E. Merrill, 1968, pp. v-xiv.
Metzger, Walter P. "Generalizations about National Character: An Analytical Essay." In Robert Merideth, ed. *American Studies: Essays on Theory and Method.* Columbus, Ohio: Charles E. Merrill, 1968, pp. 145-173.
Middleton, Thomas H. "The Great Muddling Metaphor." *Saturday Review,* June 14, 1975, p. 59.
Miller, Arthur. *Death of a Salesman.* Harmondsworth: Penguin, 1961.
Minahan, John. "Is 'Free Market' a Dirty Word? An Interview with the Secretary of the Treasury." *Saturday Review,* July 12, 1975, p. 19.
Myrdal, Gunnar. *An American Dilemma.* New York: Harper and Row, 1962.
Naether, Carl A. *Advertising to Women.* New York: Prentice-Hall, 1928.
Nessheim, Ragnhild. "På vei mot en definisjon av kulturkunnskap som grunnfagsdisiplin?" *Språk og språkundervisning,* 15, no. 4 (1982), 27-30.
Nixon, Richard. "The Long Dark Night for America Is About to End" [acceptance speech on being nominated Republican candidate for President]. *U.S. News & World Report,* August 19, 1968, pp. 54-56, 76-77.
Nye, David E. "American Studies as a Set of Discourses." *American Studies in Scandinavia,* 17, no. 2 (1985), 51-63.
Oakland, John. "British Civilisation: Institutions, Units, and Problems at Grunnfag Level." In John Oakland, ed. "Working Papers in Civilization Topics and Research," Vol. 1. Trondheim, Norway: University of Trondheim, English Institute, 1984, pp. 1-9.

BIBLIOGRAPHY 145

Oakland, John, ed. "Working Papers in Civilisation Topics and Research," Vols. 1-3. Trondheim, Norway: English Institute, Univ. of Trondheim, 1984-1986.
Olsen, Stein Haugom. "Kulturkunnskap som åndsvitenskap." In *Kulturkunnskap som forskningsfag*. Oslo: Rådet for humanistisk forskning, NAVF, 1988, pp. 25-34.
Pearce, Roy Harvey. "American Studies as a Discipline." In Robert E. Merideth, ed. *American Studies: Essays on Theory and Method*. Columbus, Ohio: Charles E. Merrill, 1968, pp. 14-25.
Pratt, Mary Louise. *Toward a Speech Act Theory of Literary Discourse*. Bloomington: Indiana University Press, 1977.
Propp, Vladimir. *Morphology of the Folktale*. Austin: University of Texas Press, 1968.
Punter, David, ed. *Introduction to Contemporary Cultural Studies*. London: Longman, 1986.
Reagan, Ronald. "State of the Union Address, January 25, 1984." In *Historic Documents of 1984*. Washington, D.C.: Congressional Quarterly, 1985, pp. 81-95.
Reagan, Ronald. "State of the Union Address, February 4, 1986." *Congressional Quarterly*, February 8, 1986, pp. 273-280.
Rehfeld, Barry. "Deal Maker." *Esquire*, 100, no. 5 (November 1983), 86-96.
Ricoeur, Paul. *The Rule of Metaphor: Multi-disciplinary Studies of the Creation of Meaning in Language*. London: Routledge and Kegan Paul, 1977.
Riesman, David, with Nathan Glazer and Reuel Denney. *The Lonely Crowd: A Study of the Changing American Character*. Garden City, N.Y: Doubleday, 1953.
Sandemose, Aksel. *Rejsen til Kørkelvik*. Copenhagen: Hans Reitzel, 1954.
Searle, John R. *Speech Acts: An Essay in the Philosophy of Language*. Cambridge: Cambridge University Press, 1969.
Searle, John R. "Indirect Speech Acts." In Peter Cole and Jerry L. Morgan, eds. *Syntax and Semantics*, vol. III: *Speech Acts*. New York: Academic Press, 1975, pp. 59-82.
Skard, Sigmund. *American Studies in Europe: Their History and Present Organization*. Philadelphia: University of Pennsylvania Press, 1958.
Sklar, Robert. "The Problem of an American Studies 'Philosophy': A Bibliography of New Directions." *American Quarterly*, 27 (August 1975), 245-262.
Skårdal, Dorothy Burton. "Kulturkunnskapens plass i engelskfaget" [Norwegian title, but English text]. *Språk og språkundervisning*, 12, no. 3 (1979), 46-54.
Smith, Henry Nash. "Can 'American Studies' Develop a Method?" In Joseph J. Kwiat and Mary C. Turpie, eds. *Studies in American Culture: Dominant Ideas and Images*. Minneapolis: University of Minnesota Press, 1960, pp. 3-15.
Smith, Henry Nash. *Virgin Land: The American West as Symbol and Myth*. Cambridge, Mass.: Harvard University Press, 1950.
Spiller, Robert E. "Value and Method in American Studies." *The Third Dimension: Studies of Literary History*. New York: Macmillan, 1964, pp. 199-216.
Spiller, Robert E. and Eric Larrabee, eds. *American Perspectives*. Cambridge: Harvard University Press, 1961
Spradley, James P. *Participant Observation*. New York: Holt, Rinehart and Winston, 1980.
Spradley, James P. *You Owe Yourself a Drunk: An Ethnography of Urban Nomads*. New York: Little, Brown, 1979.
Spradley, James P., and David McCurdy. *The Cultural Experience: Ethnography in a Complex Society*. Chicago: Science Research Associates, 1972.
Susman, Warren I. "History and the American Intellectual: Uses of a Usable Past." *American Quarterly*, 16 (1964), 243-263.
Sykes, Richard E. "American Studies and the Concept of Culture: A Theory and a Method." *American Quarterly*, 15 (Summer 1963), 253-270.
Trachtenberg, Alan. *Brooklyn Bridge: Fact and Symbol*. New York: Oxford University Press, 1965.
Trudeau, G.B. *But This War Had Such Promise*. New York: Holt, Rinehart, and Winston, 1973.
Trudgill, Peter. *Sociolinguistics: An Introduction*. Harmondsworth: Penguin, 1974.
Turner, Victor. *Dramas, Fields, and Metaphors*. Ithaca: Cornell University Press, 1974.

Tylor, Edward B. *Primitive Culture.* London: John Murray, 1920; originally published 1871.
Walker, Robert H., ed. *American Studies Abroad.* Westport, Conn.: Greenwood Press, 1975.
Walker, Robert H. *American Studies in the United States: A Survey of College Programs.* Baton Rouge: Louisiana State University Press, 1958.
Ward, John William. *Andrew Jackson: Symbol for an Age.* New York: Oxford University Press, 1953.
Warner, W. Lloyd. *Social Class in America.* Chicago: Science Research Associates, 1949.
Welter, Rush. "The History of Ideas in America: An Essay in Redefinition." In Robert Merideth, ed. *American Studies: Essays on Theory and Method.* Columbus, Ohio: Charles E. Merrill, 1968, pp. 236-253.
Whyte, William. *The Organization Man.* Harmondsworth: Penguin, 1963.
Widdowson, H.G. *Explorations in Applied Linguistics.* Oxford: Oxford University Press, 1979.
Williams, Raymond. "Base and Superstructure in Marxist Cultural Theory." *New Left Review,* 82 (November-December 1973), 3-16.
Williams, Raymond. *Culture and Society.* London: Chatto and Windus, 1958.
Williams, Raymond. *Marxism and Literature.* Oxford: Oxford University Press, 1977.
Williams, William Carlos. "This is Just to Say." *The Collected Earlier Poems of William Carlos Williams.* New York: New Directions, 1966, p. 354.
Winks, Robin W., ed. *Other Voices, Other Views: An International Collection of Essays from the Bicentennial.* Westport, Conn.: Greenwood Press, 1978.
Wise, Gene. *American Historical Explanations: A Strategy for Grounded Inquiry.* Homewood, Ill., Dorsey Press, 1973.
Wise, Gene. "The Contemporary Crisis in Intellectual History Studies." *Clio,* 5 (1975), 55-71.
Wise, Gene. "From '*American* Studies' to 'American *Culture* Studies': A Dialogue Across Generations." *Prospects,* 8 (1983), 1-10.
Wise, Gene. "'Paradigm Dramas' in American Studies: A Cultural and Institutional History of the Movement." *American Quarterly,* 31, no. 3 (1979), 293-337.
Woodiwiss, Kathleen E. *The Flame and the Flower.* New York: Avon Books, 1972.